A-Level English Language

The Revision Guide

Exam Board: AQA B

Editors: Polly Cotterill, Rob MacDonald, Jennifer Underwood

Contributors: Tony Flanagan, Heather Haynes, Rachael Powers, Chris Reynolds, Elisabeth Sanderson, Michael Southorn, Luke von Kotze, Emma Warhurst

Proofreaders: Paula Barnett, Katherine Reed

Acknowledgements

Page 19, Text B:	With thanks to iStockphoto® for permission to use the images on p.19
Page 36, Text B:	www.growingkids.co.uk
Page 45, Text B:	Jean Aitchison, The language web, 1997 © Jean Aitchison 1997, published by Cambridge University Press, reproduced with permission
Page 82, Text F:	www.allotment.org.uk

Every effort has been made to locate copyright holders and obtain permission to reproduce sources. For those sources where it has been difficult to trace the copyright holder of the work, we would be grateful for information. If any copyright holder would like to make an amendment to the acknowledgements, please notify us and we will gladly update the book at the next reprint. Thank you.

ISBN: 978 1 84762 280 8

Published by Coordination Group Publications Ltd.

Groovy website: www.cgpbooks.co.uk
Jolly bits of clipart from CorelDRAW®
Printed by Elanders Hindson Ltd, Newcastle upon Tyne.

Contents

Early Language Development

Language development is a long process, so get cracking, else you'll never get those first words out.

Language Development may Begin in the Womb

There is some evidence that suggests language development starts **before** birth.

1) **DeCasper and Spence (1986)** found that babies sucked on their dummies more when their mothers read them the **same story** that they'd also read aloud during the last six months of the pregnancy.

2) **Mehler et al (1988)** found that four-day-old French babies increased their sucking rate on a dummy, showing interest or recognition, when they heard French as opposed to Italian or English. This suggested that they had acquired some awareness of the **sounds of French** before they were born.

3) **Fitzpatrick (2002)** found that the heart rate of an unborn baby **slowed** when it heard its **mother's voice**.

> All this suggests that even in the womb, babies become familiar with the **sounds**, **rhythms** and **intonations** of language.

Babies start to use their Vocal Chords Straight Away

1) The period between birth and the first word being spoken is known as the **pre-verbal** or **pre-language** stage.

2) **Crying** is the first main vocal expression a baby makes. It makes the **caregiver** (e.g. parents, sibling, or baby-sitter) aware that the baby needs something. Crying can indicate **hunger**, **discomfort** or **pain**.

3) This isn't really a **conscious act** on the baby's part. It's more an **instinctive response** to how it feels.

Babies then start to Form Sounds — the Cooing Stage

1) At the **cooing** stage (which starts when they're **six to eight weeks old**), babies start making a **small range** of sounds — they get used to moving their lips and tongue.

2) This starts with **vowels** like /u/ and /a/. Then they start linking these to produce **extended vowel combinations** like *ooo* and *aaah*. They start to use **velar consonants** (ones made using the back part of the tongue) like /k/ and /g/ to form sounds like *coo* and *ga*.

3) These sounds don't carry any **meaning** — the baby is just **experimenting** with sounds.

4) Gradually these sounds become more **defined** and are strung together. This **vocal play** is the start of babbling.

Babbling is the next significant stage

1) Babies usually start to babble when they're about **six months** old.

2) At this stage, they start producing repeated consonant / vowel combinations like *ma-ma-ma*, *ba-ba-ba*, *ga-ga-ga*. These sounds are common in babies from many different nationalities. Repeating sounds like this is known as **reduplicated** or **canonical babbling**.

3) Sometimes these sounds are not repeated, e.g. *goo-gi-goo-ga* or *da-di-da*. This is called **variegated babbling**.

4) The **consonants** that you usually get in **reduplicated** or **variegated** babbling are: *h, w, j, p, b, m, t, d, n, k, g*.

5) Research has shown that **deaf** babies who've had some exposure to **sign language** will **babble** with their **hands** — producing consonant and vowel combinations in sign language. This suggests that babbling is an **innate activity**, which is **preprogrammed** to happen in the process of language development.

6) Most people argue that babbling is a **continuation** of the baby's experimentation with **sound creation** (cooing) rather than the production of sounds which carry **meaning**. For example, the infant may produce *dadadada* but they're not actually saying anything referring to *Dad* or *Daddy* at this stage.

7) Some people argue that babbling is the **beginning of speech**:

> **Petitto and Holowka (2002)** videoed infants and noted that most babbling came more from the **right side** of the mouth, which is controlled by the **left side** of the brain. This side of the brain is **responsible for speech production**. Their findings suggest that babbling is a form of **preliminary speech**.

Early Language Development

The **Babbling Stage** can be divided into **Two Parts**

1) When babies start to babble, the number of different **phonemes** (sounds) they produce **increases**. This is called **phonemic expansion**.

2) Later in the babbling stage, they **reduce** the number of phonemes they use (**phonemic contraction**).

3) This is the period when the baby starts to concentrate on **reproducing** the phonemes it hears in its **native language**. It **stops using** the sounds that it doesn't hear from its carers.

4) It's at this stage (about **ten months old**) that children of **different nationalities** start to sound different.

> A study at **Bristol University** in **2008** showed that babies who are exposed to different languages in the first nine months of their life are more able to pick out the sounds of these languages as they get older. This is because **phonemic contraction** has occurred less than it would if the baby had been exposed to one language only.

Infants start to show **Intonation Patterns** at the babbling stage

1) Even in the early stages of babbling (at six months) some babies will use **rhythms** that resemble the **speech patterns of adults**. There will be recognisable **intonation** in the strings of phonemes they put together.

2) For example, at the end of a babbling sequence the intonation may **rise**, mirroring the kind of intonation adults use when **asking a question**. Babies can also accompany these sounds with **gestures**, like pointing.

Babbling leads to the production of a **Child's First Words**

1) Eventually, certain **combinations** of **consonants** and **vowels** start to carry meaning. For example, a child might say *Mmm* to show that they want some more food. This is not a word in itself but it **functions** like one. These are called **proto-words**, and sometimes they're accompanied by **gestures** as well.

"AUDREY! Get this checked monstrosity off of me!"

2) Another example of a proto-word is when a child refers to a cat as /*da*/. This is still just a **sound** rather than a recognisable word, but it **refers** to an **object** and is not just a random utterance. At around **9 months** children start to sound like they're speaking their own **made-up language**. This is called **jargon**.

3) In the later stages of babbling, sound and meaning start to **come together**. At this stage, *ma-ma* does indicate *Mum* and *ka-ka* does mean *car*. This usually happens by the time the baby is **ten months old**.

Practice Questions

Q1 Outline a piece of research that suggests language development begins in the womb.

Q2 When does the cooing stage usually start?

Q3 What's it called when babies produce repeated consonant / vowel combinations?

Q4 What evidence is there to suggest that babbling is the beginning of speech?

Q5 Outline what happens in the two parts of the babbling stage.

Q6 What are proto-words?

Essay Question

Q1 With reference to research, outline the different stages that babies go through up to and including the babbling stage.

All this revision is making me go a bit ga-ga...

I don't know how babies get their tiny little heads around proto-words and extended vowel combinations. They must be smarter than they look. It's hard enough learning about them learning about this learning about... but don't mind me and my canonical babbling. Get learning all the important information on this page and you can be as clever as a baby.

Phonological and Pragmatic Development

Once babies have moved on from the babbling stage, they start trying to pronounce words. They don't always get them right first time but they can still make themselves understood. Experts claim that this is when they start to get really cute.

Phonological Development depends on the Individual

1) Children learn **vowels** and **consonants** at different speeds. They learn to use some **phonemes** earlier than others.

2) Most children will be able to use all the **vowels** in English by the time they're two-and-a-half years old.

3) They might not use all the **consonants** confidently until they're **six** or **seven** years old. The earliest consonants that they master tend to be /m/ and /n/ (known as **nasals**), and /p/, /t/, and /k/ (known as **voiceless plosives**). The last ones tend to be the /th/ sounds in words like *thought* (the /θ/ **phoneme**) and *this* (the /ð/ **phoneme**), and other sounds known as **fricatives** like /v/, /t∫/ and /dʒ/ as in <u>v</u>ery, <u>ch</u>urch and <u>j</u>ack.

4) Children find using consonants at the **beginning** of words (**word-initial**) easier than consonants at the end of words (**word-final**). For example, they'll find it easier to say the /t/ in *teddy* than the one at the end of *sit*.

Simplification helps children Communicate

1) Learning to **pronounce** things properly is difficult, but children can still **communicate** — if they can't pronounce a word as adults do, they use a simpler version. Simplification mainly applies to **consonants**.

2) There are three main kinds of phonological simplification — **deletion**, **substitution**, and **cluster reduction**:

Deletion Sometimes a child **drops** a consonant altogether, particularly at the **end** of a word. For example, they might say *ca* rather than *cat*.

Substitution Instead of dropping a consonant, a child might **replace it** with one that's easier to say. For example, they might say *wegs* rather than *legs,* or *tup* rather than *cup*.

Cluster Reduction Where there are **consonant clusters** (two or more consonants together in a word), a child may **drop one** of the consonants. For example, the child will say *geen* rather than *green*.

Berko and Brown (1960) reported what they referred to as the ***fis phenomenon***. A child referred to his plastic fish as a *fis*. When an adult asked *Is this your fis?*, the child said no, stating instead that it was his *fis*. When the adult then asked *Is this your fish?*, the child replied *Yes, my fis*.
This suggests that children can **recognise** and **understand** a **wider range** of phonemes than they can **produce**.

Other Features are common in phonological development

1) **Addition** is when a vowel is added to the end of a word, e.g. *dog* is pronounced *dogu*.

2) **Assimilation** is when one consonant in a word is changed because of the influence of another in the same word, e.g. *tub* becomes *bub* because of the influence of the final /b/.

3) **Reduplication** is when a phoneme is repeated, like *moo-moo* (for *cow*), or *bik-bik* (for *biscuit*).

4) **Voicing** is when voiceless consonants like *p, t, f, s* (sounds produced without using the vocal chords) are replaced by their voiced equivalents *b, d, v, z*, so instead of saying *sock*, a child might say *zok*.

5) **De-voicing** is when voiced consonants (sounds produced using the vocal chords as well as the mouth / tongue / lips), are replaced by their voiceless equivalents, so instead of saying *bag* a child might say *pag*.

It takes longer to Develop Intonation

1) Even at the babbling stage, babies begin to demonstrate **intonation** patterns. When they start to put words together, it becomes even more obvious, e.g. they put stress on certain words, e.g. *that's <u>mine</u>*.

2) It takes a long time for children to understand the complexities of intonation and stress. For example, **Cruttenden (1985)** found that ten-year-olds had difficulty distinguishing between:

a) *She <u>dressed</u>, and fed the <u>baby</u>* (she dressed *herself*, and fed the *baby*), **and**

b) *She <u>dressed</u> and fed the <u>baby</u>* (she dressed the *baby* and fed it too).

Lexis, Grammar and Semantics

Children start off by using one or two words to express themselves. As their vocabulary grows, they start using more and more words, and they're able to put them together to form basic grammatical relationships.

Children acquire vocabulary Very Quickly

1) This table gives you an idea of how your **vocabulary grows** as you get older:

Age	Number of Words Used
18 months	50 +
2 years	300
5 years	approx. 3000
7 years	approx. 4000

A child's ability to **understand words** will always develop quicker than their ability to **use** them. At 18 months old, a child can **actively** use 50 words, but can **understand** around 250.

The **increase** in vocabulary between age 2 to 7 is so big that these figures can only ever be an **estimation**.

2) Children's first words relate to their **immediate surroundings**. They're connected to things that children can see, hear, taste, smell and touch, or that have a **social function**. Words that express concepts and more abstract ideas start to appear as the child becomes more **self-aware** and **experiences** more of the world.

3) As they get older, children's **vocabulary** continues to **increase**, and their **grammar** becomes more **accurate** and **complex**. It's difficult to know for sure, but it's been estimated that 11-year-olds have a vocabulary of around 40 000 words.

First Words can be put into Categories

Nelson (1973) studied the first fifty words produced by eighteen children and grouped them into **five categories**:

1) **Classes of Objects** — *dog, shoe, ball, car*
2) **Specific Objects** — *Mummy, Daddy*
3) **Actions / Events** — *give, stop, go, up, where*
4) **Modifying things** — *dirty, nice, allgone*
5) **Personal / Social** — *hi, bye-bye, yes, no*

Don't tell me... don't tell me... Dog... No? Table?

Classes of **objects** formed the largest group — it's easier for children to identify things that they can actually **touch**.

Children soon learn to Use Words Creatively

When they're between 12 and 18 months old children will **improvise** if they don't know the word for something. This takes **two** main forms — **underextension** and **overextension**:

1) **Underextension** is when a child uses a word in a very **restricted way**. For example, when a child says *hat*, but means only the hat that she wears rather than any hat.

2) **Overextension** is when a child uses a word to refer to several **different** but **related** things. For example, she might use the word *cat* to refer to anything with four legs, like foxes, dogs, etc.

Rescorla (1980) said there were two types of overextension — **categorical** and **analogical**:

- **Categorical** is when a word is used to refer to things in a similar category, e.g. the word *car* is used to refer to buses, trucks and other forms of four-wheeled vehicle. This kind of overextension is most common.

- **Analogical** is when a word is used to refer to things that aren't clearly in the same category but have some **physical** or **functional relation** to each other, e.g. the word *hat* is used for anything near or connected with the head.

Aitchison (1987) suggested three other Development Processes

1) **Labelling** is when a child links a **sound** to an **object** — they are able to call something by its **correct name**.
2) **Packaging** is when a child begins to understand the **range of meaning** a word might have. They recognise that the word *bottle* can cover different shapes and sizes, but that they all have a similar **function**.
3) **Network building** is when a child starts to make **connections** between words, e.g. they understand that words have **opposites** like *big* and *small*, or know that *little* and *small* are **synonyms**.

Lexis, Grammar and Semantics

...ost first words function as Holophrases

The stage where a child says their first words is known as the **holophrastic** or **one-word stage**. Holophrases are **single words** that express a **complete idea** — an individual word performs the same function as a sentence would.

For example, when a child says *teddy*, the **meaning** of this utterance isn't obvious straight away. It could be *here's my teddy* (like a **declarative** sentence), *where's my teddy?* (an **interrogative**), *get my teddy* (**imperative**), or *here's my teddy, excellent!* (**exclamative**).

Caregivers often need **contextual clues** (e.g. being able to see the objects surrounding the child, intonation and stress) and the child's **non-verbal communication** to interpret holophrases.

The two-word stage is the Beginning of Syntax

At around **eighteen months** children start to use **two words** in **conjunction**. When they do this they automatically begin to create **grammatical relationships** between words — the start of **syntax**.

There are some common combinations:

baby crying	**subject + verb**
catch ball	**verb + object**
daddy dinner	**subject + object**
(daddy is cooking dinner)	
dolly dirty	**subject + complement**

- These combinations show **similar patterns** to more complex grammatical constructions.

- The phrases use the **basic blocks of meaning** needed for sentences (subject, verb, object and complement).

complement — gives more information about the subject or obj...

The Telegraphic Stage combines three or more words

At around **two years old**, children start to use three or four word combinations — the **telegraphic stage**.

These utterances are also formed according to **grammatical rules**:

doggy is naughty	**subject + verb + complement**
Jodie want cup	**subject + verb + object**
give mummy spoon	**verb + object + object**

- Children still focus on the words that carry **most meaning**.

- They **omit functional words** e.g. prepositions (*from, to*), auxiliary verbs (*has, do*) and determiners (*a, the*).

By **age five**, children will be able to use a **range** of **grammatical constructions** which include:

1) **Coordinating conjunctions** (like *and* and *but*) to link separate utterances.
2) **Negatives** involving the auxiliary *do* (e.g. *don't like it*).
3) **Questions** formed with *Who, Where* and *What*.
4) **Inflections** like *-ed* for past tense, *-ing* for present participles and *-s* for plurals.

...ctice Questions

...hat five categories did Nelson put first words into?
...at is overextension? Outline the two types that Rescorla identified.
...t are holophrases?
...down three common grammatical combinations that you find in the two-word stage.
...appens in the telegraphic stage?

...ren's early language acquisition with reference to the research of Nelson, Rescorla and Aitchison...

...words with lots of ho   les in the mid   dle...

...es could speak English fluently from the moment they were born? It would certainly...
...section would just be a load of blank pages at the start of a book and you'd probab...
...onderful facts on these pages and then at least you've got your money's worth.

More Grammar Acquisition

Ah, good old grammar — it always pops in to cheer you up when you're feeling a bit jaded. Have a look a[t] [the] Language Frameworks section if you need a reminder of any of the technical terms, then just sit back and e[njoy].

Inflections seem to be Acquired in a Set Order

1) Children start to **add inflections** to their words as early as **20 months old**.

2) Studies have shown that inflections are acquired in a certain order. A study by **Brown (1973)** of children aged between 20 and 36 months suggested that the **order** in which children learn inflections is as follows:

If you're a little rusty o[n] inflections and affixation, h[ave] a look at p. 60-61 in Section [...]

	Inflections	A Child Will Say (e.g.)
1	present participle -ing	I going (although am will still be missing)
2	plural -s	cups
3	possessive 's	Teddy's chair
4	articles (a, the)	get the ball
5	past tense -ed	I kicked it
6	third person singular verb ending -s	She loves me
7	auxiliary be	It is raining (or, more likely, It's raining)

3) **Katamba (1996)** found that there was **little connection** between the **frequency** with which these inflection[s are] used by parents and the **order** in which children acquire them.

4) *A* and *the* are used **most frequently**, and *-ed* **least frequently**, but they're fourth and fifth in terms of acquisition. This suggests that **imitation** doesn't have a strong influence on how children acquire inflection[s].

5) The *-ing* inflection is acquired the **earliest** — probably because it represents the **present tense**, and the chi[ld] will relate more to things happening 'now', than in the past or the future.

Inflections are Learnt in Three Stages

Cruttenden (1979) identified **three stages** in the acquisition of inflections:

Stage 1 — Inconsistent Usage
A child will use an inflection correctly **some of the time**, but this is because they've learnt the **word**, not the **grammatical rule**, e.g. they might say *I play outside* one day and *I played outside* the next.

Stage 2 — Consistent Usage but sometimes misapplied
For example, applying the regular past tense inflection *-ed* to irregular verbs. A child will say something like *I [drinked it*, rather than *I drank it*. This is called an **overgeneralisation** or a '**virtuous error**' — they understan[d how] past tense verbs are formed but **mistakenly apply** the construction to an irregular verb.

Stage 3 — Consistent Usage
This is when children are able to cope with **irregular forms successfully**, e.g. they say *mice* rather than *mouses* and *ran* rather than *runned*.

Children use grammatical rules Without Being Taught Th[em]

Children seem to acquire the grammatical rules of language just by being in an [environment where it] is spoken and where they can **interact with others**:

Berko's (1958) 'Wug' Test
1) Children were shown a picture of a strange creature and told i[t was a Wug. Then they were shown] **two of the creatures** and told 'Now there is another one. Th[ere are two...'. The idea was for] the children to complete the sentence. Three-to-four-year-o[ld...]

2) The test showed that children hadn't used the -s because they [had seen] a *Wug* before. They'd **automatically** used the **rule** that states -s is [...]

3) This is called **internalisation** — they'd heard the rule so often that it [...]

Phonological and Pragmatic Development

Children's Language has a range of Different Functions

1) At first, a child can get responses or reactions by using **proto-words**. After a while they start to use **recognisable** words, which have **different functions** depending on their context. For example, the word *dummy* could be an order (*get my dummy*), or a question (*where's my dummy?*).

2) **Halliday (1975)** states that the early language of children has **seven functions**:

Instrumental	to get something (e.g. 'go toily' meaning 'I want to go to the toilet').	
Regulatory	to make requests or give orders (e.g. 'Not your teddy' meaning 'Leave my teddy alone').	These four are about the child satisfying their social, emotional and physical needs.
Interactional	to relate to others (e.g. 'Nice Mummy').	
Personal	to convey a sense of personal identity and to express views and feelings (e.g. 'naughty doggy').	
Heuristic	to find out about the immediate environment (e.g. 'What boy doing?').	These two are about the child coming to terms with their environment and their place within it.
Imaginative	to be creative through language that relates to imaginative play, storytelling, rhymes and humour (e.g. 'One day my Daddy came home and he said...').	
Representational	to convey information (e.g. 'I'm three').	

Children quickly learn to Interact With Others

1) Babies learn about **social conventions** even before they can speak. For example, the game of "peek-a-boo" familiarises the baby with **turn-taking** and is an early form of social interaction.

2) Even at the babbling stage, a child's carer might respond to their babbling as if they were having a **conversation** — so there's some basic **interaction** between child and caregiver.

3) As a child's **pragmatic** development continues, they can interact in more **sophisticated** ways. They will **start conversations**, use a full range of **speech functions** and show **politeness features**. They start to use more adult forms of interaction like **turn-taking**, **adjacency pairs** (e.g. saying *hello* when someone says *hello* to you) and **opening and closing sequences** (e.g. *hello* and *goodbye*).

4) **Non-verbal communication** (like hand gestures and facial expressions) and **non-verbal aspects of speech** (like pitch, volume, intonation and pace) also become increasingly **sophisticated** as children grow up.

Practice Questions

Q1 Which phonemes do children usually learn to pronounce last?

Q2 Outline the three different kinds of simplification.

Q3 What is the *fis phenomenon* and what does it suggest about how children acquire language?

Q4 What is meant by assimilation in the context of language acquisition?

Q5 According to Halliday, what are the seven functions of early language? Give examples.

Essay Question

Q1 Explain the phonological features that are found in the speech of young children who haven't yet learned to pronounce all the phonemes correctly.

Phonological development — babies are always looking at their mobiles...

Ah, if only life was as simple as it used to be when you were little. Remember the good old days on the farm playing in the mud and digging for worms. Sadly life's a bit more complicated these days what with revision and exams. Don't worry though, everything you ever wanted to know about phonological development is right here on these pages. Phew.

More Grammar Acquisition

Learning to Ask Questions is a three-stage process

In the first **three** years, children develop the ability to construct **questions**.

> **Stage 1 — around 18 months**
>
> During the two-word stage, children start to use **rising intonation** to indicate a question, e.g. *Sit me?*, or *Go walk?*

> **Stage 2 — between the ages of two and three**
>
> In telegraphic talk, children continue to use rising intonation but now **include Wh- words** in the utterances, e.g. *Where tractor?* or *What Mummy doing?* As they continue to develop, they use a wider range of **interrogative pronouns**, such as *why*, *when*, and *how*.

> **Stage 3 — From the age of three upwards**
>
> Children will use what's called a **subject-verb inversion**, e.g. *Can I see it?*, or *Did she break it?*, instead of constructions like *I can see it?* They also use **auxiliary verbs** for the first time, e.g. *What is Mummy doing?*

Oscar the Grouch was never that intimidating before he went into make-up.

Negatives follow a Similar Pattern

At the same time as they start using **interrogatives** (questions), children learn to use **negatives**.

> **Stage 1 — around eighteen months**
>
> Children use *no* or *not* to make things negative, normally at the **beginning of the phrase** rather than at the end, e.g. *no juice, not baby's bed*.

> **Stage 2 — between two and three years**
>
> Children start to use *no* and *not* in front of **verbs** too, like *I no want juice* and *I not like teddy's bed*. They also develop the use of **contracted negatives** like *can't* and *don't*, e.g. *I can't drink it* and *I don't like it*. These two forms can sometimes get **mixed up**, e.g. *I can't like it*.

> **Stage 3 — from three years upwards**
>
> Children stop using *no* and *not* in the way they did in stage 1. They **standardise** their use of *can't and don't*, and start using other **negative contractions** like *didn't* and *won't*, e.g. *she didn't catch it* and *he won't build it*. The use of *isn't* usually develops **slightly later** (e.g. *Mummy isn't here*).

Practice Questions

Q1 Outline the order in which inflections are acquired. Give examples.
Q2 List Cruttenden's (1979) three stages in the acquisition of inflections.
Q3 What evidence is there to suggest that children use grammatical rules without being taught them?
Q4 What is subject-verb inversion and when do children usually start to use it?
Q5 At what age do children usually start to use contracted negatives?

Essay Question

Q1 Describe how children acquire the grammatical rules of English, with reference to appropriate research.

The examiner won't let you get away with a virtuous error...

Goodness me, they're so demanding — they want the right answers and they want them now. Well, in the exam anyway. But it's better if you get to grips with these pages sooner rather than later. That way, you can get on with the important things in life, like continuing to marvel at the thrilling twists and turns that English Language Acquisition throws at you.

Theories of Language Development

Get your fountain pen out and prime your serious face, cos here's a bit of highly intellectual, slightly dry theory. Yes, I agree that it's rather dull, but get these pages learnt and you'll be on the way to tons of lovely marks.

Behaviourists argue that Language is Acquired by Imitation

Imitation Theory

1) **Skinner (1957)** suggested that language is acquired through **imitation** and **reinforcement**:
   - Children **repeat** what they hear (imitation).
   - Caregivers **reward** a child's efforts with **praise**.
   - They also reinforce what the child says by **repeating** words and phrases back and **correcting mistakes**.
2) This approach says that children learn all the **specific pronunciations** of individual words by copying an adult — therefore in theory it explains an important part of their **phonological development**.

Problems with Imitation

There are some problems with imitation theory:

- Children can construct new sentences they've **never heard before**, so they aren't always directly **imitating**.
- They don't **memorise** thousands of sentences to use later, so their development can't be **exclusively based** on repeating what they've heard their parents or other people saying.
- Imitation can't explain **overgeneralisations**, like *he runned away* (see p. 8). Children **can't copy** these errors because adults don't make them.
- Imitation theory also **can't explain** things like the *fis* phenomenon (see p. 4) — the fact that children can **recognise** a much larger range of words than they are actually able to **use**.

Other people argue that Language Acquisition is Innate

1) **Chomsky (1965)** argued that a child's ability to acquire language was **inbuilt**. He said that language isn't taught, but it's a **natural development** that occurs when children are **exposed to language**.
2) He suggested that each child has a **Language Acquisition Device (LAD)**, which allows them to take in and **use** the grammatical rules of the language that's spoken where they live.
3) Chomsky's approach seems to explain **how** children end up making overgeneralisations and **why** they acquire inflections in a **certain order** — it's as if the brain is **preprogrammed** to make this happen.
4) Therefore children might learn language quickly because they are **predisposed** to learn it.
5) More evidence for Chomsky's theory is that **all children** pass through the same early stages of language acquisition, before **refining** their range of sounds to their native language (see p. 2-3).
6) There are some **common features** of language known as **linguistic universals**, e.g. every language contains a combination of regular and irregular verbs. This suggests that all speakers acquire language in a similar way, so it supports the idea that children have an **LAD**.
7) One criticism of Chomsky's theory is that the innate approach **underestimates** the **significance** of Skinner's argument that **interaction**, **imitation** and **reinforcement** are important in language development.

Piaget developed the Cognitive Approach

The **cognitive approach** focuses on the importance of **mental processes**. **Piaget (1896-1980)** stated that a child needs to have developed certain **mental abilities** before he or she can acquire particular aspects of language:

1) At first a child can't mentally process the concept that something can exist **outside** their **immediate surroundings**. This is called being **egocentric**.
2) By the time they're 18 months old, children realise that things have **object permanence** — they can exist all the time, even if the child can't see them. This coincides with a big increase in vocabulary (see p. 6).
3) The child is then mentally better equipped to understand **abstract** concepts like **past**, **present** and **future**.
4) One **criticism** of this approach is that it doesn't explain how some people with **learning difficulties** are still **linguistically fluent**. This suggests that **cognitive** development and **language** development aren't as **closely connected** as the cognitive approach suggests.

Theories of Language Development

Language Development needs Input from Others

The **input approach** argues that in order for language to develop there has to be **linguistic interaction** with **caregivers**.

1) **Bruner (1983)** suggests that there is a **Language Acquisition Support System (LASS)** — a system where caregivers **support** their child's linguistic development in **social situations**.

2) There are clear **patterns** of **interaction** between child and caregiver in **everyday social situations**, like meal times, bath-time and when playing. The caregiver talks to the child and encourages them to talk back by pointing things out and asking questions, e.g. *what's that there, is it a doggy?* As a result of this **linguistic support** the child gradually learns to play a more **active part** in social situations, e.g. asking the caregiver questions.

3) Children who are **deprived** of language early on don't seem able to acquire it easily later. **Lenneberg (1967)** proposed the **Critical Period Hypothesis**, which states that without linguistic interaction **before** ages 5-6, language development is **severely limited**.

4) This view is supported by some rare cases where children **without** any exposure to language in the first five years of life (e.g. cases of extreme **child abuse**) subsequently fail to develop **normal speech**.

Vygotsky presented a Socio-cultural Theory of Language Development

This theory suggests that **social interaction** and experiencing different **social and cultural contexts** are very important for language development. **Vygotsky (1978)** identified two significant factors that contribute to language development — **private speech** and the **Zone of Proximal Development (ZPD)**.

1) **Private Speech** — when a child **talks aloud** to itself. Vygotsky saw this as a major step forward in a child's mental development — this is evidence the child is **thinking for itself**.

2) **The ZPD** — when a child needs a caregiver's help in order to **interact**, e.g. if a doctor asks *Where does it hurt?*, the child might not answer. The caregiver either responds for the child or tries to encourage a response. This gives the child a **model** to apply to **similar situations** in the future when it might respond without help.

This kind of support is known as **scaffolding**. Children require it less and less once they become more able to deal with different social and cultural situations on their own.

Language Acquisition can't be explained by Just One Theory

Unfortunately, there isn't just one model of language acquisition that can **fully explain** how a child learns to speak.

1) Theories of **innate acquisition** and **cognitive developments** do not take into account the role of **interaction** in the development of a child's language.

2) Theories of **imitation** and **reinforcement** can't explain the fact that some features of language apply to **everyone**, and that all babies show similar cooing and babbling features, **regardless** of their native language.

3) The most likely explanation is that language development involves **all** of these different influences to some degree.

Practice Questions

Q1 Outline the behaviourist theory of language acquisition.
Q2 What evidence is there to suggest that all children have an LAD?
Q3 What is object permanence?
Q4 Outline Bruner's theory of the LASS.
Q5 Outline Vygotsky's socio-cultural theory of language development.

Essay Question

Q1 "Children acquire language through imitation and reinforcement." How far do you agree with this statement? Your answer should refer to the benefits and drawbacks of specific linguistic theories.

Surely only boys have LADs...

Welcome, child. Many brave souls have hacked through the Forbidden Forest to reach the mystical land of Kwebegon. And many brave souls have been taken. For it is written in the stars that only one will conquer the dreaded Borsidone Beast and reach the Zone of Proximal Development. Open your mind, and prepare to enter. Just watch your head on the scaffolding...

Social Interaction

You might have thought that kids aren't very skilled in the delicate art of social interaction, but actually, tantrums in supermarkets are just their way of interacting with the general public. Well, they've got to practise somewhere.

Caregivers *Talk* to children in a *Particular Way*

1)   This kind of language is referred to as **child-directed speech** (CDS), **caretaker speech**, or even **motherese**.

2)   The language features of CDS are often **simplified** or **exaggerated** and often have the purpose of **encouraging** a child to **interact** as they're easier to understand.

Child-directed Speech *has* Distinctive Linguistic Features

Phonology and Prosody

1)   **Intonation** is exaggerated and words are **stressed** more strongly than they are in adult conversation, e.g. stress on *good* in *What a good girl you are, Annie.* The **pitch** is usually **higher**.

2)   Words and phrases are **repeated**, e.g. *Get the ball, Annie, get the ball.*

3)   The **pace** is often much **slower**, with **longer pauses** than in adult speech.

Lexis

1)   **Vocabulary** is often **simplified**, e.g. instead of saying *banana*, a parent might say *nana* instead.

2)   Caregivers use **reduplication** (see p. 2) — constructions like *choo-choo*, *din-din*, or *moo-moo*.

3)   They also use **diminutives** — like *birdie*, *doggie* or *fishy*.

4)   A high proportion of words will refer to objects that the child can **see** and **touch** e.g. *Look at the pussy-cat, Annie, it's playing with the ball.*

Grammar

1)   **Sentence structures** are simplified, and **function words** (e.g. auxiliary verbs) are often **omitted**. E.g. instead of saying *Annie, shall we go for a walk?*, a caregiver might say *Annie go for walk?*

2)   **Proper nouns** (including frequent **repetition** of the child's name) are often used instead of pronouns, e.g. instead of *Are you making a sandcastle?* a parent will say *Is Annie making a sandcastle?* A higher proportion of nouns will be **concrete nouns** (e.g. *cup, apple, bottle*).

3)   The **present tense** will be used more than the past tense. The caregiver will talk more about what's **happening 'now'** e.g. *Are you singing?* rather than in the past e.g. *Were you singing yesterday?*

Caregivers *use* Techniques *to* Encourage Language Development

1)   They **repeat** certain **structures**, e.g. *Annie get the tractor, Annie wash the baby, Annie find the bottle.*

2)   They ask lots of **questions**, e.g. *Annie, where's doggie gone?, Have you got a poorly hand?, Is Sally crying, Annie?* This **encourages** the child to **respond**.

3)   They use lots of **imperatives**, e.g. *pick up dolly, eat din-dins, drink milk.*

4)   Caregivers often **expand** on what the child has said:

> **Mother:** *What you doing, Annie?*
> **Child:** *Playing.*
> **Mother:** *Yes, you're playing with your car.*

5)   They also **recast** what the child has said, re-presenting information in a **different way**:

> **Mother:** *What you doing, Annie?*
> **Child:** *Playing with my car.*
> **Mother:** *Yes, that's your car, isn't it?*

No one really knows if *CDS* has any *Impact* on Development

1)   Child-directed speech isn't used by parents in **every culture**, but speakers of all cultures grow up to be **fluent**.

2)   There's **nothing conclusive** to suggest that CDS does or doesn't work — research has produced conflicting results.

3)   It could be that CDS is more about **building a relationship** than about language development in particular.

Social Interaction

Children learn how to **Interact** with their **Caregivers**...

Caregivers use **CDS** to **encourage** children to **respond** and teach them about how **dialogue** works.

1) The **early** conversations that children have (at around **age two**) are usually **initiated** and **maintained** by **adults**.

2) They tend to be made up of **short statements** by the child that the **adult** responds to — the child **doesn't** really **respond** to what the adult says. For example:

> **Father:** *Look at the ducks, Annie, can you see the ducks?*
> **Child:** *Quack quack.*
> **Father:** *That's right the ducks go quack quack don't they?*
> **Child:** *In the water.*

3) Children **develop** a lot between the ages of **two** and **four**. They start to understand **turn-taking** and take part in **dialogues**. They start to **understand** the **needs** of the **listener** — they learn to give appropriate **answers** to questions and to **respond** in a way that can **initiate** a **further response** from the other speaker.

4) They also develop more **awareness** of **social factors** in conversations, e.g. they begin to understand when to use **politeness forms** like *please* and *thank you*.

5) They become better at getting someone's **attention**, e.g. they use **adverbs** like *well* to show that they have something to say. They also start to use **people's names** to get their attention.

6) **Starting school** or **nursery** has a big **impact** on **social interaction skills**, as children meet **more people**. They develop more awareness of what **kind** of **language** is **appropriate** in certain **contexts**, e.g. they start to use more **formal** language in the **classroom** compared to the **playground**.

...and with **Other Children**

At around the age of **two** children also start to have **conversations** with **each other**.

1) These **early conversations** are **limited** because at this age the children only have a **lexis** of about **300 words**.

2) They're known as **closed conversations** because there's no **progression** in them. The speakers don't have the **skills** to make **meaningful responses**, so they can't keep the conversation going. The conversations are made up of **short statements**:

> **Child A:** *I got sweeties.*
> **Child B:** *Nice sweeties.*
> **Child A:** *I got big bag.*

As they get **older**, children's use of **lexis** and **grammar** increases, so they're able to have more **complex** conversations.

1) They develop **pragmatic skills** — they learn to use language to **form relationships** with each other, and to try and **get** what they **want**. This can involve **repetition**, e.g. *Can I have the pen now? Can I have the pen now?* and **persuasive tactics**, e.g. *If you don't give me it then I won't be your friend.*

2) They also **imitate** adult speech and develop more **awareness** of the **type** of **language** that's **appropriate** for different **audiences**, e.g. **older** children often use **CDS** when they're talking to **younger** children.

Practice Questions

Q1 List three grammatical features of child-directed speech.

Q2 How do conversations between children and their caregivers change as children get older?

Q3 Why are most two year olds only able to have closed conversations with each other?

Essay Question

Q1 "The main aim of CDS is to encourage the child to respond." To what extent do you agree with this statement?

Does ikkle babba think CDS is annoying? Oo yes he do, yes he do...

When I was at primary school most of our assemblies seemed to be about the story of Louis Braille (the man who invented Braille...). After one such assembly the head asked if anyone had any questions, and Ashley Ross in Year One stuck his hand up and said "My mummy bakes pizzas". Aww, see — knowing the right thing to say in a situation isn't as easy as it sounds...

Learning to Read

If you're reading this now then I can pretty much guarantee that you must have been taught how to read at school. And it's a good thing too, cos now you get to read all about how you learnt to read in the first place. Yay.

There are **Different Approaches** to **Teaching Children** to **Read**

There are **three** major **approaches** to the teaching of **reading**:

1 The phonics approach

- This approach involves looking at **letters** and **letter combinations** in terms of **sounds** (reading '**by ear**'), e.g. *cow* is separated into the phonemes /c/ and /ow/. It means that children can **sound out** unfamiliar words.
- It's **useful** for words like *latch* that are **pronounced** as they're written, but is **less useful** for words like *through*.
- The approach has also been **criticised** because it just **focuses** on **sounds** and **letters**, rather than on the **meanings** of the words.

2 The "look and say" approach

- This is also known as the **whole word** approach. It involves **recognising** whole words by **sight** alone, **rather** than **breaking** them down into **separate phonemes** (reading '**by eye**').
- It focuses on the **meaning** of words, and teaches children to recognise **common** words like *and, see, went* etc.
- However, relying on this method requires children to **memorise** a **large number** of words, and **doesn't** give them the **skills** to **work out** the **sound** or **meaning** of **unfamiliar** words.

3 The psycholinguistics approach

- This approach sees reading as a **natural development** that comes from being in an **environment** where books are **read**, **valued** and **available**.
- It's an **active approach** to reading — the **reader** is given **responsibility** for **working out** what a word **means**, rather than just being **told** the meaning.
- When children come across a word they **can't** read, they're encouraged to **work out** the **meaning** by looking at the **rest** of the **sentence** and other **clues** like **illustrations**.
- The idea is to encourage children to **focus** on **meaning**, rather than just working out **symbols**. It's also designed to make them aware of the **importance** of **context**.
- However, the approach has been **criticised** because it leaves a lot to **chance**.

Teachers tend to use a **Combination** of **Approaches**

Over the past **sixty years**, there's been a lot of **debate** about which method for teaching reading is **best**.

1) Schools tend to use a **combination** of **approaches** rather than just rely on one. This is because some children **respond** better to one method than another.

2) It also ensures that children develop a **range** of **skills**. The **phonics approach** teaches them to recognise **symbols**, while the **look and say** and **psycholinguistics approaches** teach the importance of **meaning** and **context**.

3) It's also really **important** that children **practise** reading **outside** of **school** — some researchers see this as the **most important** factor in **improving** a child's reading ability.

Techniques for **Developing Reading Skills** depend on the **Child's Age**

1) Up to age **five**, caregivers may **read** stories and nursery rhymes to children, and help children enjoy the **physical experience** of books, e.g. turning pages, pointing to letters and saying the sounds out loud.

2) Between **five** and **six**, caregivers / teachers will read them fiction and non-fiction, get them to **break down** words into individual sounds (**phonemes**), and get them to **match sounds** to **letters**.

3) Between **six** and **seven**, they'll get children to **read aloud**, set classroom tasks involving speaking, interacting and reading, and encourage them to **talk** about what they've read.

4) Between **seven** and **eight**, they may introduce children to **different genres** and provide them with the chance to **discuss** different aspects of what they've read.

Or, here's an idea. How about you TURN YOUR OWN PAGE AND STOP BEING SO LAZY.

Learning to Read

Reading *Develops* in *Stages* as you go through school

Obviously, everyone progresses at different rates, but there are some **general stages** that **most children** pass through.

Pre-school (up to age 5)	• Kids take part in activities that **prepare** them for reading, e.g. playing with bricks, jigsaws, and matching pictures. This helps them distinguish between **different sizes**, **shapes** and **patterns**. In turn this prepares them for identifying **letters** and **combinations of letters**. • They can turn pages in books themselves and verbally **create** their own **stories**. • They begin to identify some **individual letters**, such as the first letter of their name, and also begin to match some **sounds** to letters.
Between five and six years old	• They **increase** the number of **letter-sound** matches that they know. • They realise that in English, letters on a page move from **left** to **right** and **top** to **bottom**. • They begin to **recognise** frequently used words.
Between six and seven years old	• They can read stories they're **familiar** with. • They use a range of **reading strategies** — when they're stuck on a word they may use the context to guess what it is, or sound it out **phonetically**. • They recognise more and more words just **by sight**. • They **break down** words into individual **sounds** to read an unfamiliar word. • They start to read with some **fluency**.
Between seven and eight years old	• They read more **fluently**, and their **vocabulary** continues to increase. • They use reading strategies **accurately** (such as **predicting** what words might come next). • They're better at working through **individual sounds** to read unfamiliar words.

Reading *Skills* carry on *Developing After* you've learnt to read

The learning process **continues** for a long time **after** children are first able to read **fluently**. Up until about the age of **18**, their reading continues to **improve** and their **vocabulary** grows:

- They become **familiar** with a **wider range** of texts.
- They **read to learn** — their reading improves enough that they can use texts to find out **information**.
- They're able to use more **complex** and **varied** texts to find out information **without help**.
- They read in **different ways** for **different reasons**, e.g. for work and for pleasure.

1) Some children's progress stops here — they're able to read fluently, but they never reach a stage where they can **interpret** what they're reading **critically**.

2) This is often because they **stop reading** apart from when they **have** to.

3) Other children's reading **continues** to **improve**, until they're able to **analyse** and **criticise** what they're reading. This means they can **select** the most **important** points from a text and **develop** their own **opinions** about them.

Practice Questions

Q1 Outline one criticism of the "look and say" approach.

Q2 What does the psycholinguistics approach to teaching reading involve?

Q3 Outline what most children are able to do in terms of reading at a pre-school age.

Q4 How do a child's reading skills continue to improve after the age of 8?

Essay Question

Q1 With reference to the three main approaches to teaching reading, explain why it's often thought to be best to teach a combination of approaches.

Psycholinguistics — not something you'd think would be encouraged...

Seeing the whole process of learning to read set out in a big table like that has made me realise just how much work goes into it. It's amazing to think that at one point I was a little pipsqueak who struggled with the alphabet, and now I'm a fully fledged reader who can understand all the letters and some whole words. My parents are very proud, but they hide it well...

Learning to Write

As if learning to read wasn't enough, the poor little mites have to learn to write too, even though they'd probably much rather be having a nice little nap or a biscuit. It hardly seems fair, but it does come in handy I suppose.

Writing develops in Stages

1) Children go through **stages** of **development** before they can write and spell entire words. Although they need to be able to **recognise** letters and words before they can write, they seem to learn to write **alongside** learning to read.

2) When young children do **drawings** they're actually starting to learn the **motor skills** (coordination) they'll need for **writing**.

3) As their **motor skills** develop, children are able to learn the **conventions** of written language, e.g. **spelling**, **punctuation** and **layout**.

4) How **quickly** a child learns to write depends on how much **practice** they have, e.g. whether they're given crayons to use before they start school. It also depends on the child's **intelligence**, and how much they've been exposed to **role models** who write.

5) Theorists have **different ideas** about how many stages are involved in learning to write, and how old children are when they go through them.

After eating 74 crayons Gabi's writing had started to suffer.

Barclay (1996) outlined 7 Stages of Writing Development

Stage 1 **Scribbling**	Kids make random marks on the page, which **aren't related** to letters or words. They're **learning the skill** of keeping hold of a pencil or crayon, which prepares them for writing. They often **talk** about what they're scribbling.
Stage 2 **Mock Handwriting**	Children practise drawing **shapes** on paper, although it's still not usually possible to work out what the drawing represents. Letter-like forms (**pseudo-letters**) begin to appear in or with drawings as the first sign of **emergent writing** — an attempt to write letters.
Stage 3 **Mock Letters**	Children produce **random letters**, but there's still no awareness of spacing or of matching **sounds** with **symbols**.
Stage 4 **Conventional Letters**	Children start matching **sounds** with **symbols** — writing down letters that match the sounds being heard or spoken. Words are unlikely to be spaced out. Children start using **initial consonants** to **represent words**, e.g. *h* for *horse*. The initial letter might be read out as if the **full word** is there on the page.
Stage 5 **Invented Spelling**	Most words are spelled **phonetically**, though some simple and familiar words are spelled correctly.
Stage 6 **Appropriate Spelling**	Sentences become more **complex** as the child becomes more aware of standard spelling patterns. Writing becomes more **legible**.
Stage 7 **Correct Spelling**	Most words are spelled **correctly**. Older children have usually started to use joined-up writing, too.

Learning to Write

Kroll (1981) outlined *4 Stages* of *Writing Development*

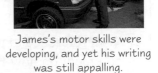

James's motor skills were developing, and yet his writing was still appalling.

1) The Preparatory Stage — from 18 months

- Children develop the **motor skills** needed for writing.
- They begin to learn the basics of the **spelling system**.

2) The Consolidation Stage — 6-8 years

- Children **write** in the same way as they **speak**.
- They use lots of **colloquialisms**.
- They use **short declarative statements** and **familiar conjunctions** like "and".
- They won't yet be sure how to **finish** off a sentence.
- They begin to express ideas in the form of **sentences**, though without much punctuation.

3) The Differentiation Stage — age 8 to mid-teens

- Children become aware of the **difference** between the **conventions** of **spoken** and **written** language.
- They begin to understand that there are **different genres**, for example letters and stories.
- They begin to **structure** their work using writing **guides** and **frameworks**.
- They use **more complex grammar** and **sentence structures**.
- **Punctuation** becomes more **accurate** and **consistent**.

> Every child develops at a different rate, so this is just a rough outline of how old they are at each stage.

4) The Integration Stage — mid-teens upwards

- Writing becomes more **accurate**, with a **wider vocabulary** and more **accurate spelling**.
- Children understand that **style** can **change** according to **audience** and **purpose**.
- **Narrative** and **descriptive** skills improve. They write expanded stories, with **developed characters**, a **plot** and a **setting**.
- They develop a **personal writing style**. This continues to develop throughout **adulthood**.

Practice Questions

Q1   How do scribbling and drawing help prepare young children for writing?

Q2   Name two factors that can affect how quickly a child learns to write.

Q3   What is emergent writing?

Q4   According to Barclay (1996), what happens in stage 6 of learning to write?

Q5   According to Kroll (1981), what happens in the consolidation stage?

Q6   According to Kroll (1981), what skills do children develop in the differentiation stage?

Q7   According to Kroll (1981), in which stage do children develop a personal writing style?

Essay Question

Q1   Children go through different stages of development when they learn to write. Outline what happens with reference to one theorist in particular.

One day I woke up and I decided to revise and it was very nice...

There's another stage — the 'learning to write about learning to write' stage. And you reach that stage at the exact age you are today. What a happy coincidence. Anyway, it's the end of the section — hurrah. To celebrate, why not go back to your childhood by getting the squirty cream out the fridge and squirting it straight into your mouth until it inflates like a big toad.

Sources and Exam Questions

Now have a go at this practice exam question.

Text A is a transcript of an interaction between a three-year-old and her mother.
They are looking at an illustrated story book.

Text B is an extract from the story book.

1. With reference to the texts and knowledge from your study of language acquisition,
   comment on how Ellie is being helped to understand what happens in the story. *[48 marks]*

Text A — Conversation between Ellie (aged 3 years) and her mother

Ellie:	she's in her bed
Mum:	no look (.) look she's got out of bed now
Ellie:	why
Mum:	well let's see (.) she jumped out of bed and stretched her arms as wide as she could
Ellie:	// ooh
Mum:	can you do a big stretch Ellie (2) that's it (.) ooh <u>very</u> wide (1) and look can you see what colour curtains she's got
Ellie:	curtains
Mum:	yes (.) she's got <u>green</u> curtains like you have in your room (.) hasn't she
Ellie:	there's got (.) I've got green curtains and she's gotted green curtains
Mum:	that's right (.) she's got green curtains (.) clever girl
Ellie:	and she's got water
Mum:	ooh is that the next page (.) yes you're right she's all wet isn't she (.) she's gone to wash her face
Ellie:	wash her in the water
Mum:	in the water (1) she went into the bathroom to wash her face and look (.) <u>splish</u> <u>splash</u> <u>splosh</u> (.) can you say that darling (.) splish
Ellie:	plish
Mum:	splish
Ellie:	and in there there's bubbles in there
Mum:	ooh yes look at all the bubbles in the sink (.) and she's getting all wet isn't she
Ellie:	what is it on the next one
Mum:	okay let's see (.) on the next one (.) can you see what she's doing
Ellie:	she's got her
Mum:	what's that in her hand
Ellie:	she's got her (.) toothbrush
Mum:	<u>very</u> good (.) she's cleaning her toothypegs isn't she
Ellie:	she's bushing them
Mum:	that's right (.) you <u>brush</u> your teeth don't you (1) shall we read it (.) Rosie squeezed out a <u>big dollop</u> of toothpaste and brushed her teeth
Ellie:	I can't see her teeth
Mum:	no but she's got a big smile hasn't she (.) look (.) <u>big wide</u> smile

Transcription Key	
(.)	*Micropause*
(2)	*Pause in seconds*
//	*Interruption / overlap*
<u>underlining</u>	*Emphasis*

Text B — Extract from an illustrated children's story

Rosie jumped out of bed and stretched her arms as wide as she could. She liked to have a big stretch every morning.

Then she went into the bathroom to wash her face. Splish, splash splosh! "Washing your face is fun," thought Rosie.

After she had washed her face, Rosie squeezed out a big dollop of toothpaste and brushed her teeth.

Lexical Change

These pages are all about how the words we use change over time. You might have noticed this happening yourself — if you started this book saying 'I will revise,' I bet it's now changed to 'I can't be bothered...'

New Words have been created throughout History

New words are **always** being **created**.

1) For example, people think that Shakespeare invented over **1700 words**, some of which are still used today, including *assassination*, *courtship* and *submerged*.

2) In recent years the following new words have been accepted into the Oxford English Dictionary: *fashionista*, *wussy* and *twonk* (a stupid or foolish person).

3) The **creation** of new words is known as **coinage** and the new words themselves are called **neologisms**.

Hank didn't know it, but he was seconds away from coining 'flame-grilled steak'.

New Words are Created in Different Ways

There are many **different ways** of forming new words. Here are some of the methods:

Borrowing	A simple way to create new words is to 'borrow' a word from **another language**. Many of the words used frequently in everyday language are **borrowings** or **loan words**. For example, *barbecue* comes from **Spanish**, *bungalow* comes from **Hindustani** and *robot* comes from **Czech**. A lot of borrowings relate to **food** or **objects** not traditionally found in the UK, e.g. *spaghetti* from **Italian**.
Scientific Progress	Advances in **medicine**, **science** and **technology** cause new words and phrases to be invented. For example, *in vitro fertilisation* is a term that emerged in the **1970s**.
Affixation	Words can also be created by **affixation**, where **new prefixes** or **suffixes** are added to existing words. Many words in the English language have been created by adding **Latin** or **Greek prefixes** or **suffixes**. For example, the **Greek** word *hyper* is found in the words *hyperactive*, *hypersensitive* and *hypertension*.
Compounding	Sometimes a new word is created by **combining** two separate words to create one word. This is known as **compounding**. For example, *thumb* can be **combined** with *print* to create *thumbprint* and *hand* can be combined with *bag* to create *handbag*.
Blending	**Blending** is when two separate words are actually **merged together**. For example, *netiquette* is a **blend** of *net* and *etiquette*. Similarly, *infotainment* is a blend of *information* and *entertainment* and *satnav* is a blend of *satellite* and *navigation*.
Conversion	New words are also created when an existing word **changes class**. This is known as **conversion**. For example, many words that started off as **nouns** are now also used as **verbs**: *text/to text*, *chair/to chair* (a meeting), *mail/to mail*. Note that the word **doesn't** change its **form** (it looks the same), only its **function** (it does a different job).

New Words can also be created by Different Forms of Shortening

1) **Clipping** — this is when you drop one or more syllables to create an **abbreviation**. For example, *demo* is often used rather than *demonstration* and, more recently, *rents* rather than *parents*. Abbreviations are a common form of **word creation**.

2) **Initialism** — this is where the **first letter** of a word **stands for** the word itself. For example, *FBI* takes the first letters of the words in *Federal Bureau of Investigation*, *OTT* takes the first letters of *over the top*, and *FYI* takes the first letters of *for your information*. **Initialisms** are always pronounced **letter by letter**.

3) **Acronyms** — **initial letters** of words also **combine** to **create** a completely **new word**. For example, *NASA* stands for *National Aeronautics and Space Administration* and is pronounced as a word in itself rather than letter by letter. The acronym *WAGS* refers to the **wives and girlfriends** of footballers.

4) **Back-formation** — this is a **less frequent** form of word creation. It occurs when a word looks like it has been created by adding a **suffix** to an existing word, but actually, the suffix has been **removed** to create the new term. For example, the noun *baby-sitter* came **before** the verb *baby-sit*, *word-processor* came before *word-process*, *burglar* came before *burgle*, and the verb *enthuse* is a back-formation of *enthusiasm*.

Lexical Change

Many **New Words** come from the **Names** of **People, Places** or **Things**

1) **Words** can also be **derived** from people's **names**. Words that develop in this way are known as **eponyms**. For example, the word *nicotine* comes from **Jean Nicot**, a French ambassador to Portugal in the sixteenth century who sent **tobacco seeds** back to France.

2) **Brand names** are a source of new words too. Two examples (both taken from American English) might be asking for something to be *Xeroxed* rather than *photocopied* or asking for a *Kleenex®* rather than a *tissue*.

3) Sometimes words are derived from a particular **place**. For example the word *limousine* derives from **Limousin** (a French province). This came about because the car's designers thought the shape of the driver's compartment was **similar** to the kind of hoods historically worn by shepherds in that area.

Words can Disappear

1) Just as new words enter the language, old words **disappear**. Words that have become **obsolete** (are no longer used) are known as **archaisms**. For example, these words aren't used any more in modern English: *durst* (dare), *trow* (think).

2) Other words might still be used, but have fallen out of fashion, e.g. *courting* (dating), *wireless* (radio).

"No, grandpa, I'm not courting. I'm just using him for his private jet..."

English Spelling hasn't always been fixed either

The English spelling system (its **orthography**) is notoriously complicated and is actually quite random — although you might expect this from a language that has borrowed words from almost everywhere.

The letters *-ough* are probably the most famous example of a segment that can represent a lot of **different sounds** in spoken English. The spelling of words with *ough* originated in **Middle English**, but probably sounded something like the *-och* part of *loch*. Here are a few **variations**:

through (an 'oo' sound)	*though* (an 'oh' sound)	*tough* ('uff')
cough ('off')	*plough* ('ow')	*hiccough* ('up')

One reason for **idiosyncrasies** like this is that changes in **pronunciation** occurred **during** and **after** standardisation of the spelling system. This meant sounds were lost from spoken English, while their **original historic spellings remained** in written English.

Practice Questions

Q1   What is a neologism? Suggest three ways they can be formed.

Q2   What is affixation? Give an example.

Q3   Explain what back-formation is and give an example.

Essay Question

Q1   Describe the ways in which different forms of shortening can be used to create new words.

All this cramulation is shoodling my thoughtbox...

Personally, I can't think of a Shakespeare play that takes place under water, but he must have had a reason for inventing the word 'submerged.' Maybe Juliet drowned in the first draft of R&J — he was probably right to scrap that idea, bit tacky, don't you think? Anyway, learn how words come and go over time, and pass me the wireless from betwixt those knaves yonder.

Semantic Change

Here's an idea — try thinking of this section in life cycle terms. The previous two pages covered the birth and death of words. It's a bit sad, but don't worry — these pages are about the lucky words that manage to get reincarnated...

Semantic Change is when a word's Meaning Changes

1) Words which **remain** part of a language for many years often **change their meaning** over time. This is known as **semantic change**.

2) Language **changes** all the time without you really noticing, e.g. **metaphors** like *surfing the net* are now used without thinking, as are words like *rip* (to copy from a CD), *burn* (to copy files to a CD) and *cut* (a record).

3) **Slang** and **colloquialisms** give **new meanings** to **established words**. For example, the following words are used to **express approval**: *cool, buzzing, safe, mint*.

A word can Develop a more Positive or Negative Meaning

Amelioration

1) Amelioration is when a word develops a more **positive meaning**.

2) For example, *nice* used to mean *foolish*. *Tremendous* used to mean *terrible* but is now used to say something is *very good*. *Mischievous* used to mean *disastrous* but now means *playfully malicious*.

Pejoration

1) Pejoration is when a word **develops** a **negative meaning**.

2) For example, *hussy* used to have the same meaning as *housewife* but now refers to *an impudent woman of loose morals*. *Notorious* used to mean *widely known* but has come to be associated with being **well known** for **doing something bad**.

1) Some words change their meaning **altogether**. For example, *tomboy* used to mean a *rude, boisterous boy* but is now only used to refer to girls who act in what is perceived to be a **boyish way**. *Porridge* used to refer to *soup containing meat and vegetables* but now means *cereal made of oatmeal and milk*. *Bimbo* was originally a term for *fellow* or *chap*. It then took on negative connotations and came to mean *stupid man* before eventually being a term aimed **exclusively** at **women**.

2) Sometimes a word ends up making **less** of an **impact** than it used to. This is known as **weakening**. For example, the word *terrible* used to mean *causing terror* but now it's used to say that something is **very bad**. *Glad* used to mean *bright, shining, joyous* but now it means *pleased*.

The Meaning of a word can get Broader or Narrower

1) A word that has a **specific meaning** can develop a **broader meaning** over time. This process is known as **broadening, generalisation, expansion** or **extension**.

2) For example, the word *bird* used to mean a *young bird* or *fledgling* but now refers to **birds in general**. *Place* used to refer to an *open space in a city, market place, or square* but now means a *portion of space* anywhere. *Arrive* used to be a term that was connected with *landing on shore* after a long voyage. Today, it means to come to the end of any kind of journey, or to **reach a conclusion** (*I have finally <u>arrived</u> at a decision*).

Who are you calling 'girl'?

3) A word that has a general meaning can develop a **narrower meaning**. This process is called **narrowing, specialisation** or **restriction**. For example, the word *meat* used to mean *food* in general but now specifically refers to *animal flesh*. *Girl* was a term used to refer to a *young person* generally and *liquor* used to mean *liquid* but now refers to *alcoholic drink* specifically. You still see the old meaning of *liquor* in a cooking context, e.g. you cook something then *pour off the liquor*.

4) Words can go though **multiple semantic changes**, e.g. *silly*:

> **Silly:**   *blessed > innocent > pitiable > weak > foolish*

Semantic Change

Political Correctness can Cause Semantic Change

1) In the last thirty years, **political correctness** has had a major impact on how language is used. Its purpose has been to **remove** words and phrases that have **negative connotations** from the language.

2) For example, *old people* are referred to as *senior citizens*, and *disabled people* as *people with disabilities*. The term *half-caste* is no longer used for people who are *mixed race*.

3) **Trivialising suffixes** such as *–ess* and *–ette* are **no longer used** in many cases. The word *actor*, for example, now refers to either a **male or female performer** and the word *actress* is gradually becoming **redundant**.

4) Many people feel these types of **semantic change** are **positive** and that they remove negative connotations from the language. However, some people feel it's gone a bit too far when the changes begin to **obscure meaning**, e.g. using the job title *sanitation consultant* instead of *toilet cleaner*.

Figurative Expressions give New Meanings to Old Words

METAPHOR

1) Metaphors describe things as if they were actually **something else**.

2) For example, the following phrases were originally associated with the sea, but are now used metaphorically: *plain sailing, high and dry, clear the decks*.

METONYMY

1) Metonymy is when we use a word **associated** with an **object** instead of the object's actual name.

2) For example, *cash* used to mean *money box* but over time it came to mean the **money itself**.

IDIOM

1) Idioms are **sayings** that don't make sense if you **literally interpret** the meanings of the words.

2) E.g. you **can't tell** from the words alone that *it's raining cats and dogs* means *it's raining very heavily*.

3) Idioms **don't appear** out of **nowhere**. They usually have some **factual**, **literary** or **historical** basis.

4) For example, the expression *to have a chip on your shoulder* comes from nineteenth century America. A young man would challenge others to a fight by inviting them to knock a wood-chip off his shoulder.

EUPHEMISM

1) Euphemism is the use of **alternative** words or phrases to **avoid offending** someone or to make something **appear less unpleasant**.

2) E.g. there are lots of euphemisms for **death**, like *kicking the bucket, pushing up daisies*, or *popping your clogs*.

CLICHÉ

1) If idioms are used a lot, they may become **clichés** — **overused phrases** which fail to excite the imagination.

2) The **business world** has many **clichés**, such as *pushing the envelope* and *blue-sky thinking*.

Practice Questions

Q1 Explain the terms amelioration, pejoration and weakening, giving an example for each one.

Q2 What do narrowing and broadening mean?

Q3 How do metaphor, metonymy and euphemism contribute to semantic change?

Essay Question

Q1 Giving examples, discuss the impact that political correctness has had on semantic change.

Where do words go if they want to get narrower? Word Watchers...

It's all fun and games, this, isn't it? If you don't know what kind of figurative expression that last sentence is, go back and read these two pages all over again. Twice. As for me, I'm off to invent myself a new job title. Maybe I could be a 'Learning Aid Perfectioning Operative,' a 'Revision Expert' or, as someone has just kindly suggested, an 'office monkey.' Nice.

Grammatical Change

Just as you thought it might be safe to nod off on your desk for a few minutes and have a little dribble, here's some grammar to slap you round the face and rouse you from your lovely slumber. It's a hard life, isn't it...

The way words are **Formed** is **Always Changing**

Here are some of the biggest grammatical changes that happened to **Late Modern English** — English since 1700:

Verbs

1) The **past tense** of some **irregular verbs** used to be formed differently — over time the **stem vowels** have changed, e.g. the verb *spake* has become *spoke* in PDE (Present Day English).

2) **Auxiliary verbs** (e.g. *do*) started to be used more in Late Modern English (English from 1700). This had an effect on **word order** (see below).

Adjectives

1) **Comparative** and **superlative** inflections (i.e. *greater* and *greatest*) exist in PDE as they did before. However, in the **nineteenth century** superlatives like *properest* were also **grammatically acceptable**. In PDE you'd use *most proper* instead.

2) The two ways of forming comparatives and superlatives could also be **combined**, e.g. you could use **double comparatives** like *more cleverer*. In PDE it's enough to use *more clever* or *cleverer*.

Nouns

1) The way that nouns are used in sentences has changed less than other word classes, although they were **capitalised** more frequently until the 18th century (see p. 28).

2) One change is that the **definite article** is now used less often with certain nouns, e.g. constructions like *the Russian* to mean Russians in general, and *the Sciatica* (back pain) would now be replaced with *Russians* and *sciatica*.

Syntax used to be more **Complex**

Since 1700, there's been a trend towards **sentences** being **shorter** and **syntax** has become **less complicated**.

Sentences used to contain a lot more **subordinate clauses**. For example, there are **three** subordinate clauses in this sentence (shown with square brackets) from an 1886 novel by Thomas Hardy:

What was really peculiar, [however,] [in this couple's progress,] [and would have attracted the attention of any casual observer otherwise disposed to overlook them,] was the perfect silence they preserved.

PDE tends to use **simpler punctuation** — there are **fewer commas** and **semicolons**. This makes it seem **less formal**.

Word Order has also **Changed**

Use of **auxiliary verbs** (like *do*, *have*, *be*) has **increased**. This has had an impact on **word order**.

Interrogatives

1) Interrogatives didn't always include auxiliary verbs. In Early Modern English (from around 1500-1700) they were formed with the **verb** at the **start**, so the order was **verb-subject-object** (V-S-O). You might still see this in **Late Modern English** texts:

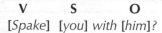

V	S	O
[*Spake*]	[*you*]	with [*him*]?

2) In PDE, interrogatives are often formed using an **auxiliary verb**, and the **subject** and **main verb** are **inverted** from the old construction to S-V-O. Auxiliary verbs like *do* are now used at the **start** of the question:

Auxiliary	S	V	O
[*Did*]	[*you*]	[*speak*]	with [*him*]?

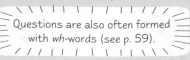
Questions are also often formed with *wh*-words (see p. 59).

Negative Constructions

1) In PDE, the negative *not* is placed **before** the verb rather than after it.

2) A '**dummy auxiliary**' is used (an auxiliary verb like *do* that isn't really necessary for the meaning of the phrase to be understood).

3) For example, phrases like *I <u>do</u> not deny it* have **replaced** older constructions like *I deny it <u>not</u>*.

Grammatical Change

Contractions *have gone* **In** *and* **Out** *of* **Fashion**

1) By the **early 18th century**, **contractions** had become very common in written and spoken English.

2) This was partly because they were often used in **poetry** to make sure that words fit the **metre** of the verse. It was also because **printers** contracted words to make them fit on the line. This meant that the use of contractions was **inconsistent**, often within the same printed text.

> - Contractions that are still used in PDE were common in the early 18th century e.g. *can't, would've, she'll*.
> - Others were also used, e.g. *'twas* (it was), *o'er* (over), *e'en* (even).
> - **Proclitic** contractions are used less in PDE. This is when the contracted part of the word is at the beginning, e.g. *'tis*. In PDE there are more **enclitic** contractions, where the contracted part of the word comes at the end, e.g. *it's*.
> - **Past participles** used to be contracted, to show that the final syllable wasn't pronounced, e.g. *disturb'd, defer'd*.

3) However, **18th century** writers like **Jonathan Swift** complained that contractions were 'corrupting' English — they were **inelegant**, and would make the language very difficult for future generations to understand.

4) This **backlash** against contractions led to them going **out of fashion**. By the **19th century** they were much less common. For example, this is an extract from a letter written in 1866 by the Victorian writer Wilkie Collins (words that would have probably been contracted in the 18th century are underlined):
   I am unfortunately already engaged to dinner on Sunday — or *I should have* been delighted to dine...

5) Contractions then started to be used more frequently in the second half of the **20th century**. It's normal to see them used in **printed texts** (like this one), although you don't always see them in very **formal** texts.

Double Negatives *used to be* **Common** *in English*

> 1) Today, **double negatives** such as *I don't want nothing* are considered **non-standard**.
>
> 2) The authors of 18th century **prescriptive grammar books** (see p. 30) tried to standardise and 'improve' English. They decided that double negatives were 'incorrect' and shouldn't be used.
>
> 3) The grammarian Robert Lowth used **mathematical logic** to argue that double negatives weren't acceptable: *"Two negatives in English destroy one another, or are equivalent to an affirmative,"* i.e. they make a **positive**.

The **Function** *of* **Words** *can change over time*

1) As people use more and more **new technology** like mobile phones and the Internet, the **function** of some words associated with it has changed — **nouns** like *text, email* and *Facebook®* have become **verbs**.

2) Some **adjectives** are now used instead of **adverbs**, e.g. *I'm good* instead of *I'm well*. This is an American usage that has become common in British English.

3) In **Standard English**, the adverb *well* is used with **past participles**, e.g. *the meal was <u>well</u> cooked*. In contemporary English it's also common to see *well* as an intensifying adverb before an **adjective**, e.g. *that was <u>well</u> good*.

4) *Innit* used to be a shortened version of the **tag question** *isn't it?* In **urban slang** it's become interchangeable with a **variety** of other tag questions too, e.g. *we can do that tomorrow <u>innit</u>?* where *innit* means *can't we?*

5) In the 1990s the **intensifying adverb** *so* started to be used with not, e.g. *I'm <u>so</u> not ready for this*.

Practice Questions

Q1 Give an example of how word order has changed since 1700.

Q2 Give three examples of grammatical change since 1900.

Essay Question

Q1 Describe the main features of grammatical change in English since 1700.

I've just had the most horrible cold — it was a superlative infection...

You'd think that the fact that grammar is constantly changing would make it a bit more exciting. Poof! There goes the complex syntax — vanished forever. Bang! Here's the all-new dummy auxiliary. It promises so much, and yet in reality it's about as interesting as fourteen rice cakes and a kilogram of houmous. Tastier, but no more inspiring.

Phonological Change

Phonology is the study of sounds in a language. Phonological changes affect the pronunciation of individual sounds, which can help explain how and why certain sounds are acquired or lost over time.

Pronunciation is Always Changing

1) The most **significant shift** in pronunciation occurred between 1400 and 1600. During this period the **long vowels** of Middle English changed a lot. This transition is called the **Great Vowel Shift**.

2) Between **1700** and **1900**, the long *a* vowel sound in words such as *path* (pronounced *parth*) came to be used in **southern parts** of Britain. Before this it would have been pronounced in its **shorter form**, as it is in **Northern** and **Midlands** accents.

3) In Present Day English (**PDE**), the **schwa** ([ə]), is a **generic vowel sound** we use instead of **fully pronouncing** the vowel. It's become more common in **everyday speech** than it used to be, even in **RP** (Received Pronunciation — see p. 27). For example, we tend to say *uhbout* rather than **a**-bout, and *balunce* rather than *balance*.

4) **Consonants** have also changed. For example, before the nineteenth century, *-ing* was generally pronounced *in*, (as it is in many regional accents today), even by the **middle** and **upper** classes.

5) Today, some speakers **replace** the *th* sound with *f* (saying *fink* rather than *think*, or *vem* rather than *them*). This is a feature of **Estuary English** (see p. 27) called **th-fronting**.

Intonation Patterns have also changed over time

1) A specific change in intonation since the early 1990s is **uptalk** or **upspeak**. Usually, intonation **rises** when people ask a question. With uptalk, intonation rises when you're **making a statement**.

2) The following sentences demonstrate how uptalk might come across in conversation:

> I was going to town? And I saw this man? He was acting really strange? Then he came up to me? Asked me for a cigarette?

3) At first uptalk was a feature of **teenage speech**, but it's now found in a **wider range** of age groups.

4) One theory is that it's been picked up from **Australian intonation patterns** that are heard in soaps like *Neighbours* and *Home and Away*.

5) There are different theories about people's **reasons** for using it. Some linguists say it's used because speakers don't want to sound **aggressive** or too sure of themselves. Others claim that it's only used when speakers are telling someone **new information**.

Pronunciation changes for Lots of Reasons

1) **Social factors** can affect pronunciation — people often change the way they talk depending on the **context** and who they're talking to.

2) Your pronunciation probably changes when you're being formally **interviewed**, compared to when you're talking with **friends**, e.g. you might be more **careful** about pronouncing *h*s in words like *how* and *have*. This is known as **upward convergence** — making everyday language sound closer to **RP**:

> A study in Norwich by **Trudgill (1983)** showed that women were more likely to speak closer to RP when they knew their language was being observed.

3) **American English** has also affected British English pronunciation. For example, the traditional British English pronunciation of *harass* stresses the **first syllable** (*harass*), but in PDE people might stress the **second syllable** (*harass*), as in American English.

4) The **media** can influence pronunciation. The BBC has a **Pronunciation Unit** which guides broadcasters on how to pronounce words. This is to make sure that the presenters are **consistent**, but **viewers** then often **copy** the pronunciation of **unfamiliar** or **foreign** words, and they become seen as the **standard** pronunciation.

5) **Aitchison (1991)** suggests that phonological change is a **process**. First, the accent of one group differs from that of another. The second group is **influenced** by the pronunciation of the first group, a **new accent** emerges and the process continues.

Phonological Change

Received Pronunciation *has changed significantly*

1) **Received Pronunciation (RP)** was seen as the standard English accent and is sometimes called the **Queen's** English. It's a **prestige** accent — it's associated with a good standing in **society** and with being **well-educated**.

2) The emergence of RP in the **twentieth century** also caused **regional accents** to be seen as socially inferior.

3) RP was adopted as the **official accent of the BBC** in 1922, because they thought it was the accent that everyone would be able to **understand**. This added to its **prestige value** — as all the news and public broadcasts were in RP, it became the accent of **authority**. This is why RP is also sometimes called **BBC English**.

Stephen only bought the book so Maureen would stop RPing on about her crossword.

4) From the late **1950s onwards**, RP changed quite significantly. For example, in RP before the 1960s the word *hand* was pronounced more like *hend*, *often* was pronounced more like *awften* and *tissue* was pronounced as *tisyu*.

5) In the 1960s, with **working-class** teenagers going to **university** in larger numbers and the emergence of **celebrities** who spoke with **regional accents**, RP lost some of its desirability. Emerging pop stars, actors and artists had regional accents (e.g. Paul McCartney, Mick Jagger), and young speakers wanted to **imitate** them.

6) Today, RP has been **toned down** and is rarely heard. For example, broadcasters will use **Standard English** when they are speaking, but might have a **regional accent** rather than RP.

New Accents *have emerged*

Nowadays very **few** people actually use **RP** in its 'original' form. Even the Queen's accent has changed a bit from when she was first crowned over 50 years ago.

Estuary English

1) Some linguists claim that **RP** is being replaced as the most 'acceptable' English accent by **Estuary English**. This is an **accent** that has roots in the speech found around the **Thames Estuary** area in **London**.

2) It contains many similar features to the **Cockney** accent, e.g. dropping *h*s at the beginning of words (pronouncing *hit* like *it*), and pronouncing *th* like *f* (so *tooth* becomes *toof*). For example, estuary speakers will use a **glottal stop** instead of *t*, so *bottle* is pronounced *bo-ul*. They'll pronounce *tune* as *choon* rather than *tyune*, *wall* as *waw* and *north as norf*.

3) It's used by a lot of people in the **entertainment industry**, as it's seen as a **commercially acceptable** accent.

4) Because of the **influence** of the **media**, Estuary English is becoming quite common **outside** London. You can't necessarily tell where someone's from if they use Estuary English — it's become a **widespread accent**, probably a result of people **copying** the speech of **radio** and **TV presenters**.

Practice Questions

Q1 What is the *schwa*? Give an example of when it's heard.

Q2 What is Received Pronunciation?

Q3 What is Estuary English? Give three examples of how an Estuary English speaker's pronunciation would differ from that of an RP speaker.

Essay Question

Q1 Discuss some of the reasons why English pronunciation has changed.

So there are vese free pieces of string, right...

And they're trying to get into a bar. But the door policy is 'strictly no pieces of string allowed'. So one piece of string says to his mates, "Leave this to me lads, I'll get us in". He folds his arms, ruffles up his hair and walks to the door. The bouncers see him and ask, "Hang on, aren't you a piece of string?" And he says, "No, I'm a frayed knot." Phonology — always hilarious.

Graphological Change

As if looking at words wasn't enough, graphology involves things like layout, typeface (what you might normally call 'font') and handwriting. It's about how the visual features of a text can have an impact on the overall meaning.

The Appearance of Letters has Changed over Time

Texts written hundreds of years ago look very **different** from modern day texts. This is partly because the way that some of the **letters** are written has changed.

1) From the **17th century** onwards the letter *s* was often written as ʃ (like an *f* without the cross-bar), e.g. ʃit instead of *sit*. This was based on the **handwriting style** of the period, and it appeared like this in **printed texts** until the early **19th century**, so you might see it in texts from that period. It wasn't written as ʃ if it was at the end of a word though, and was often written alongside an *s* if a word contained a double *s*, e.g. claʃses.

2) Until the **18th century** more words began with **capital letters** than they do in Present Day English. Words were capitalised if they were at the start of a sentence or if they were proper nouns (as in PDE). However, **abstract nouns** and any other word that the writer wanted to **emphasise** could also be capitalised.

Typefaces have also changed:

1) Up to the middle of the twentieth century, **serif** typefaces were usually used. They have a fine 'stroke' attached to the tops and bottoms of letters.

2) From the mid-twentieth century onwards **sans-serif typefaces** (ones **without serifs**) became fashionable.

3) Typefaces with serifs tend to seem **traditional**, while sans-serif typefaces look more **modern**.

4) Modern **printed material** has a wider range of typefaces than in the past. Print advertising, newspapers, leaflets, posters, and books will use different fonts for **different purposes**.

5) For example, *The Sun* newspaper mainly uses a **sans-serif** typeface for **headlines**, and **serif** typefaces for **articles**. It also uses a wide **variety** of **typefaces** in the headlines on its entertainment and gossip pages to attract attention and make the pages **visually stimulating**.

A — serif
A — sans-serif

Newspaper Layout has Changed

Newspaper designs have **changed** a lot in the last 100 years.

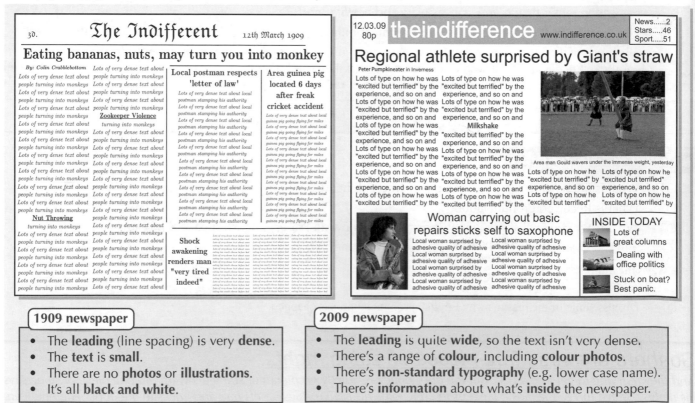

1909 newspaper
- The **leading** (line spacing) is very **dense**.
- The **text** is **small**.
- There are no **photos** or **illustrations**.
- It's all **black and white**.

2009 newspaper
- The **leading** is quite **wide**, so the text isn't very dense.
- There's a range of **colour**, including **colour photos**.
- There's **non-standard typography** (e.g. lower case name).
- There's **information** about what's **inside** the newspaper.

Graphological Change

Magazine Layout *has also* Changed

1) Modern magazines are very different from those of the eighteenth century.

2) In the past, the front page of a men's magazine, e.g. *The Gentleman's Magazine (1736)*, consisted of a **decorative illustration** at the top of the page, a title and then two **dense** blocks of print, black on white.

3) In contrast, the cover of a **modern** men's magazine such as *FHM* has a full page **glossy photograph** in the background. This is **overlaid** with print, indicating the main features to be found inside the magazine. The print has different **font types**, **colours**, and some of the text is presented in unconventional angles and styles.

The editors were less than impressed with Paul's choice of 'long legged stunner'.

The graphology of Modern Books *is* Varied

1) The earliest books often had **two columns** to a page, justified text and large margins for making notes. Modern books, like novels and textbooks, tend to have **one column** of print.

2) However, modern books can show a great deal of **variety** in terms of **layout**, **typeface** and **colour**. Non-fiction books in particular often show a lot of **innovation** and **creativity** with **colour** and **graphics**.

3) In children's books you might see blocks of print at **unusual angles**, and different **shapes** of text boxes (e.g. circles or speech bubbles). There's often a variety of **font colours** and **background colours**, and sometimes text **superimposed** on **background images**.

Electronic Media *has changed the appearance of* Written Communication

1) **Electronic media** allows writers and publishers to be more **creative** with graphology.

2) Web developers can use different **layouts**, **typefaces** and **colours** without having to think about printing costs. Web pages tend to contain **small chunks** of text broken up with **headings**, **subheadings** and **links** because this is **easier to read** on screen.

3) Web pages can also incorporate **animated text** and **images**. **Audio** is also used as part of **interactive videos**, **games** and **adverts**.

4) **Word-processing software** has given ordinary people access to loads of different **typefaces** and styles. You can **choose** which style to use depending on the **purpose** of the writing, for example:

> This is Times New Roman PS   This is Litterbox ICG

5) You'd use these typefaces to create **different effects**. For example, you might use Times New Roman PS if you were writing a serious newspaper article, and Litterbox ICG in a text for children.

6) **Mobile phones** have also had an impact on **graphology**. People can send photos and videos along with small amounts of text, which often contains features like abbreviations, numbers and emoticons.

Practice Questions

Q1   What is graphology?

Q2   Outline three ways in which the graphology of newspapers has changed over the last 100 years.

Q3   How do books today differ from the first printed books in terms of typeface and layout?

Essay Question

Q1   Describe the impact of electronic media on the graphology of the English language.

Just remember to label your axes...

X and Y — along the corridor and up the stairs. That's pretty much all the maths I remember — something to do with people living in houses made of graphs I think. It all sounds hideously impractical. The squares on that graph paper are too small even for a box room, let alone an open plan kitchen-diner. Still, mathematicians aren't exactly known for their logic, are they...

English from 1700

The biggest thing to happen to Late Modern English (1700-present) was that it became much more standardised. However, the standardisation process had actually started centuries earlier, so you need a bit of background first.

The **Printing Press** helped to **Standardise English**

1) In 1476, **William Caxton** established the first **printing press**. It was an important step towards **standardisation**. Producing **identical copies** of a text meant that everyone was reading the **same** thing, written the same way.

2) However, it was pretty tricky for Caxton. Words were often spelled **differently** according to **dialect** or the **personal choice** of the writer, so he had to **decide** which **spellings** to use.

3) He chose the type of English being used in the **courts**, the **universities** (particularly Cambridge) and in **London** at the time.

4) This dialect was already associated with **political authority**, **learning** and **commerce**. Using it in printed books gave it a feeling of **permanence** and **prestige**.

5) English became **standardised** to a certain extent, but there was still a lot of **variation** in printed texts.

6) In the **18th century** the 'state' of the language became a great concern for some writers and grammarians. They worried that because English wasn't governed by a strict set of rules, it was **decaying**. Dictionaries and **grammar books** telling people how to use English 'properly' were published and became very **popular**.

The first **Dictionaries** had a strong influence on **Standardising Spelling**

One of the most important publications in the history of English was Samuel Johnson's *A Dictionary of the English Language (1755)*, which contained about 40,000 words.

1) **Johnson's** *Dictionary* laid down rules for the **spelling** and **meanings** of words. It wasn't the first English dictionary, but it was definitely the **biggest** at the time.

2) Johnson backed up his definitions with **quotes** from 'the best writers', e.g. Shakespeare and Milton. He also provided the **etymology** of words (how they entered the language). Other English dictionaries have since used the **same method**, e.g. the OED (see p. 39). This shows how **influential** Johnson's dictionary was.

3) He said that his aim was to **record** the language — that he wanted 'not to **form**, but **register**' English.

4) However, he also stated that he wanted to **tame** the language because he felt that it was **out of control**. This is a more **prescriptivist view** (see below).

5) The dictionary was so important because it helped **standardise spelling** and **meaning**. If someone needed to know the meaning of a word or how to spell it, the dictionary could be used as a standard **reference point**.

Prescriptive Books had a major impact on **Grammar**

Prescriptivism is an **attitude** towards language that assumes there are a set of 'correct' **linguistic rules** that English should follow (see p. 38).

1) Although **grammar books** had existed since the 16th century, they became really **popular** in the **18th century**, when they were written to lay down **rules** about language and **prescribe** the **correct usage**.

2) For example, a rule that's still taught today is that *whom* should be used when *who* is the **object** of the sentence:

'Incorrect'	'Correct'
Who did you see today?	**Whom** did you see today?

3) 18th century **grammarians** were also **proscriptivists** — they outlined rules on the types of language people **shouldn't** use (while **prescriptivism** involves stating what types of language people **should** use). For example, one **proscriptive rule** states that sentences **shouldn't end** with a **preposition**, e.g. the sentence *where do you come from?* should be *from where do you come?*

4) A lot of these rules were **invented** by 18th century grammarians like **Robert Lowth**, who wrote *A Short Introduction to English Grammar (1762)*. Some were imposed on English from **Latin** or **Ancient Greek**, because these were seen as **superior languages** — they weren't spoken any more, so they couldn't 'decay' like English could.

English from 1700

The Lexis continued to Grow

1) The expansion of the **British Empire** led to words being **borrowed** from the countries that came under British rule. For example, these **loan words** came from **India**: *bangle* (1787), *dinghy* (1810) and *thug* (1810).

2) During the Late Modern period, advances in **science** and **medicine** led to the invention of new words like: *centigrade* (1812), *biology* (1819), *laryngitis* (1822), *antibiotic* (1894), *chemotherapy* (1907), *penicillin* (1929), *quark* (1964) and *bulimia* (1976).

3) **New inventions** brought more **new words and phrases** into the dictionary such as *typewriter* (1868), *motor car* (1895), *radio* (1907), *video game* (1973) and *podcasting* (2008).

4) **Social**, **cultural** and **political developments** have contributed to the **lexis** (vocabulary), e.g. *hippie* (1965), *airhead* (1972), *grunge* (1980s), and *credit crunch* (2000s).

5) New words also emerged through **international conflict** and **war** — *Blighty* (to refer to Britain, 1914-18), *blitz* (1939), and *kamikaze* (1945).

Accents and Dialects changed in the Twentieth Century

Improved **communication** and increased **mobility** in the Late Modern period (from 1700 onwards) meant that people were exposed to a **wide range** of accents and dialects for the **first time**.

COMMUNICATION

- Radio, films and television have affected regional pronunciation.

- For example, **Estuary English** (see p. 27) is a relatively new accent that is **spreading**, partly because it's used by a lot of people on **TV** and the **radio**. It originated in south-east England and London, but some people think it's **influenced speakers** as far away as Glasgow and Manchester.

- **International** soap operas (e.g. Neighbours) may have affected **younger speakers'** accents, too.

- Inventions like the **telephone** have meant that people from **different regions** can communicate much more easily.

Misinterpreting "Push here for change", Jim imprisoned six innocent people.

MOBILITY

- The invention of the **railway** and **cars** meant that people began to **travel** more around Britain. This means that **regional dialects** aren't as **self-contained**, so they're becoming '**diluted**'.

- **Very strong accents** have tended to get **softer**, so people from different regions can understand each other better than they could.

- **International travel** has also affected English. **Non-native** speakers from different countries use Standard English or American English to **communicate** with each other and with **native** English speakers (see p. 33-34).

Practice Questions

Q1 What influence did Johnson's dictionary have on spelling?

Q2 Give three examples of how grammarians became more prescriptivist in the Late Modern period.

Q3 Which factors contributed to the expansion of vocabulary during the Late Modern period? Give examples.

Q4 Explain how and why regional accents and dialects have changed since 1700.

Essay Question

Q1 Discuss how advances in transport, technology, science and medicine affected English in the Late Modern Period.

Prescriptive English — for standard eyes only...

You might remember a Blackadder episode where Johnson turns up with his dictionary. You might also remember Blackadder throwing in some words like 'pericombobulation', as if they were real words that Johnson had overlooked. Think that's funny? Just imagine what a pain it would be if you'd spent years on the dictionary only to find you'd forgotten to include "knitting".

Causes of Language Change

The last few pages have covered the ways that language can change, but unfortunately it's never really down to just one single reason. These two pages bring all the different causes together, making them 24 carat essay gold.

Language change can be **Internal** or **External**

1) **External** language change is a result of **outside influences** on a group of speakers. For example, English has been influenced by things like **invasions**, **immigration** and the **media**.

2) **Internal change** happens because of a need for **simplification** and **ease of articulation**. For example, **inflections** like *-eth* may have died out because the meaning was still clear when they weren't used, so they gradually became **unnecessary**.

Phonological Change tends to make **Pronunciation Easier**

Omission and **assimilation** are **trends** of phonological change that make things easier to pronounce.

Omission

1) Omission is when sounds are gradually **lost** from the language, because speakers **stop pronouncing** them.

2) For example, in about the last fifty years, **RP** speakers have dropped the *y* sound in words like *tune*, which used to be pronounced *tyune*. It now sounds more like *choon*.

Assimilation

1) Assimilation is where one sound in a word is affected by an **adjacent sound** to produce a new pronunciation, e.g. some people pronounce the word *sandwich* as *samwich*.

2) Assimilation also occurs across **word boundaries**, e.g. *What do you want* / *whatju want* or *Get it?* / *geddit?*

Standardisation caused a lot of **Change**

SPELLING

1) The first major development was **Caxton's printing press (1476)**. It helped to establish the medieval **East Midlands dialect** as the 'standard', as well as making texts more **readily available** to people.

2) However, there was still quite a lot of variation with spelling for the next few centuries, and it wasn't until the eighteenth century that spelling began to look fully standardised. **Johnson's *A Dictionary of the English Language*** (see p. 30) laid a firm foundation for the spelling system we have today.

GRAMMAR

1) People tried to standardise grammar in the eighteenth century. A number of scholars published books **prescribing** how English should be **constructed**, e.g. **Robert Lowth's *A Short Introduction to English Grammar* (1762)** (see p. 38).

2) These ideas have influenced what people consider to be 'good' English. This has meant that there's **less variety** in Standard English.

PHONOLOGY

1) Teaching a standardised form of **pronunciation** was a key feature of private school education. The main person behind this was the actor and educator **Thomas Sheridan** in the **mid-eighteenth century**.

2) He believed there was a **correct** way to speak and that this could be acquired through **elocution** lessons.

3) Like the other prescriptivists, Sheridan published books, including *A General Dictionary of the English Language* in **1780**, which outlined how to pronounce words 'properly'.

Technology has influenced language change

1) **Industrialisation** in the eighteenth and nineteenth centuries introduced new words and phrases relating to labour, such as *productivity*, *shift work*, and *clocking-on*.

2) **Scientific advancement**, **new inventions** and **brand names** have resulted in new words entering the language (e.g. *spacesuit*, *microwave*, *PC*, *chatroom*, *MSN®*, *email*, *download*, *hard drive*, *web page*).

It took Margaret a while to get the hang of phonetic spelling.

Causes of Language Change

Other Languages have Influenced English language change

A lot of language change has been brought about by the **influence** of **foreign languages**, especially because of **loan words** (**borrowings**). The table below shows just **some** of the languages that have influenced English over the centuries.

Period	Influence	Examples
8th-11th centuries — invasions from other countries.	Scandinavian	*skirt, cog, skip*
	French	*accompany, department, tax*
16th-17th centuries — words brought into English from Latin and Greek by writers.	Latin	*benefit, temperature, the prefixes sub and trans*
	Greek	*catastrophe, pneumonia,* the affixes *auto and pan*
18th-19th centuries — words borrowed from colonised countries during the expansion of the British Empire.	Malay	*amok*
	Hindi	*shampoo*
20th century — immigration to the UK.	Cantonese	*wok*

American English has had a Big Impact

1) In the 20th century, **America** developed into a **superpower**. Its **political**, **economic** and **cultural influence** has maintained the importance of **English** as a **world language**.

2) **American English** can be accessed all over the world, especially because of the influence of **music**, **films** and **TV**. American **brand names** are **internationally recognised** due to the influence of **advertising**.

3) **Standard American English** has a few specific lexical, grammatical and orthographical (spelling) differences from **Standard English**. For example:

Lexis	
American	**British**
trash	rubbish
sidewalk	pavement
soccer	football
gas	petrol

American Grammar
- More frequent use of the **subjunctive**, e.g. *I wish I were taller* instead of *I wish I was taller*.
- Omission of *on* in reference to days of the week, e.g. *see you Tuesday* instead of *see you on Tuesday*.
- Noun phrases ordered differently, e.g. *a half hour* instead of *half an hour*.

Orthography	
American	**British**
meter	metre
color	colour
organize	organise
gray	grey

Practice Questions

Q1 What's the difference between internal and external language change?
Q2 Explain the terms omission and assimilation in the context of language change.
Q3 What have been the major factors in the standardisation of English?
Q4 What impact have science and technology had on the language we use today?
Q5 Why has American English been such an influence on Present Day English? How do they differ?

Essay Question

Q1 Describe how standardisation, technology, and the influence of other languages have contributed to language change.

Learning all this stuff might seem like a bit of omission...

But if you like, I'll give you a-ssimilation of how it should be done. See that section on standardisation? Read it. Then cover it up. There are two points on spelling, two on grammar and three on phonology. Write them down... did you get them all right? Excellent. Well done. But 'tis only a fraction of this double page spread, so eyes down and look in for the rest...

English in the Future

I knew you would turn to this page today. Now look closer, and I will reveal the terrifying truth about what English will be like in the future. But first, you must cross my palm with silver... No? Well, it was worth a try I suppose.

English has an Uncertain Future

1) English has the **fourth highest** number of **native speakers** in the world.

2) More people speak it as a **second language** than any other language, and this number is **growing** all the time.

3) With so many people speaking English, there are **various possibilities** for how the language will change in the **future**.

English might become more Uniform

1) It's necessary for **international trade** to have a **lingua franca** (a language that people from different countries can all understand). English has taken this role.

2) As well as this, some **countries** (such as Nigeria) that weren't originally English-speaking have adopted English as their **official language**. They feel that it's necessary to have a **standardised language** that **everybody** in the country can **understand**. This has happened especially in countries that have a lot of different **tribal languages**.

3) This shows a **trend** towards **uniformity**, and it suggests that eventually some other languages may **die out**.

> 1) **American English** may become the **global standard** (the variety of English spoken by everyone in the world). It's already the **dominant** form, and the number of English speakers is **increasing**. People want to learn American English because it's the language of **world trade** and has global **prestige** and **authority**.
>
> 2) American English is also **growing** because of the global presence of American **films**, **music** and **brands** (see p. 33). As more people in less economically developed countries gain access to **TV** and the **internet**, they'll have **more exposure** to American English, so they'll be more likely to use it.
>
> 3) As the **importance** of American English grows, other varieties might **lose status** and gradually die out. This is called **dialect levelling**.
>
> 4) **Differences** between world **varieties** of English are **decreasing**. It's possible that one day this will lead to the emergence of a **World Standard English** — one that becomes the **official international language** of business and takes the place of all other varieties.

Technology might help make English more Uniform

1) English has been established as the language of **scientific** and **technological advancement** for a long time, so it's been an important language for **foreign scientists** and **academics** to learn.

2) The **internet** has spread English even further. It's been estimated that **90%** of computers connected to the internet are in **English-speaking** countries. Because of this, around **80%** of the **information** stored on computers **worldwide** is in **English**.

Janet was thrilled. Finally she could combine her two loves — technology and uniforms.

3) Technology has already had a dramatic impact on English usage. Computer software usually uses **American spelling**, such as *programs* and *fav<u>o</u>rites*. This is helping to establish American English as a **global standard**.

4) Computers are **changing** English in other ways too, for example:

- **Spell check** programmes mean people don't need to know how to spell unusual words **correctly**. This could lead to less emphasis being put on **teaching spelling** at **school**, because it isn't considered necessary.
- **Web addresses** don't contain **capital letters**, so they might gradually **die out** in **other written texts**.
- **Punctuation** isn't needed when you look something up on a **search engine**, so some marks might **die out**.

5) As **internet access** grows around the world, more people will have access to this **electronic variety** of English, so it could end up being the **World Standard English** that everyone uses.

English in the Future

English might become more Diverse

1) Another possibility is that different **varieties** of English around the world could develop into **separate languages**, e.g. American English would be completely different from Indian English. This is what happened to **Latin**, which was once spoken across a lot of **Europe**, but then **split** into **romance languages** like **Italian**, **French** and **Spanish**.

2) These separate varieties of English could then become a way of displaying **national identity** and **independence**. People might see it as a way of **rejecting cultural imperialism** from countries like America and Britain.

3) As the varieties became more different from each other, **localised national standard Englishes** might emerge, e.g. a particular form of Indian English. These forms of the standard would then become the **official language** of the country, rather than Standard English or Standard American English.

4) As well as this, **America's** economic, political and cultural **dominance** might be **challenged** by countries like **China** or **India** in the future. If this happens, then American English might not be the most useful or powerful language to learn any more.

Technology might make English more Diverse

1) English isn't the only language of the internet. As more people in **less economically developed countries** gain **internet access**, English might stop **dominating** the web. As **online translation software** improves, people won't have to be able to speak English to look at British or American websites. As well as this, there are already lots of versions of American and British websites and search engines in **other languages**.

2) Countries like **India** and **China** are likely to have much more of an impact on **science** and **technology** in the future. This could mean that languages like **Mandarin Chinese** become more important to learn than English.

If you're writing an essay about the impact of technology on the future of English, you can make it more balanced by discussing both the arguments for technology making English more diverse, and the arguments for technology making English more uniform on p. 34.

Bidialectism means speaking Two Dialects

1) Another thing that could happen in the future is that people will be able to **switch** from one **dialect** of English to the **standard**, depending on the **context** and **purpose**. Switching between two dialects is **bidialectism**.

2) This scenario imagines the possibility that **standard** forms of English will become more **uniform**, while **regional** and **social** varieties will become more **diverse**. People will have to learn the **standard** form for **formal** situations and for communicating with people from **other countries**.

3) This is **already happening** to a certain extent. For example, a Nigerian business executive might use a **regional** form of Nigerian English when speaking **informally** with **local** customers, but use a more standard English or American form with **international** customers.

Practice Questions

Q1 What is a lingua franca?

Q2 What factors might help American English become the global standard?

Q3 How might the internet lead to greater uniformity in English?

Q4 What is bidialectism?

Essay Question

Q1 'The strength of English as a world language is set to grow and grow.' How far do you agree with this statement?

In the future we won't need English — we'll just read each other's minds...

Oh, English. Just like Pocahontas, you must choose your path. One may be steady, like the river. The other may be rapid and exciting, like the river... This isn't really working out. Perhaps Pocahontas wasn't the best comparison to use. Basically what I'm trying to say is that no one knows where English is going in the future, so just learn the different arguments and move on.

Sources and Exam Questions

Here are some exam-style questions, with sources like the ones you'll get in the real paper.

Text A is from *The First Book of Manners* (1856), a guide to polite behaviour for young people.
Text B is taken from a page of a modern website, www.growingkids.co.uk, which offers advice to parents about their children.

1. With reference to both texts, comment on what they show about changes in written language over time.

[48 marks]

Text A — from *The First Book of Manners* (1856), by Felix Urban

When the hour for meals draws nigh, take care to be ready, properly dressed and washed, so as not to be behind time; it is a breach of manners to keep others waiting.

Shew no unbecoming haste to sit down; but take your place as you are desired. Wait until a blessing has been asked: the head of the family (or a clergyman, when present) usually does this; not unfrequently, however, the youngest present is called upon: should it be your duty, perform it reverently, with a due feeling of devotion, remembering that it is the offering up of a solemn prayer to Almighty God.

It is not proper to sit either so close to the table as to touch it with the body, nor too far back; the right distance is that at which the wrists can rest naturally upon the table's edge.

Sit upright, not throwing yourself back, nor yet sitting upon the edge of the chair. To place the elbows on the table, is a most unmannerly act. When a table-napkin is put for you, unfold it, and place it securely before you upon your knees.

You will find the knife and spoon at your right hand, and the fork at your left; they are to be so used.

It is unmannerly to ask to be helped before others, or to shew signs of impatience by moving about the plate or the body; such behaviour may be ascribed to greediness. Await your turn; be assured you will not be forgotten.

Text B — from www.growingkids.co.uk/TableManners.html

If a child has an assigned seat, it is easy for him/her to get into the routine of eating at the table from the moment they sit down. When comfortable and calm, encourage children old enough to eat at the table to:

·   Scoot their chair in so that they can easily reach the table without having to rest their elbows on it.

·   Put their napkins in their laps, not tucked into their shirts.

·   Understand that their plate is in the middle, forks are to the left and knives/spoons are to the right.

·   Know that their glass is up to the right of their plate.

Chow Down

When it's time to eat, even the most mild mannered of children can turn into ravenous monsters! Ask your children to:

·   Politely request the dish they would like to spoon onto their plate (if you have not already served them).

·   Serve food onto their plates using the serving utensils provided, not their own utensils.

·   Serve only one helping of food at a time. Assure your children there will be seconds if they so desire.

·   Give each foodstuff a separate space on the plate. Piling a plate with a mountain of food is a recipe for frustrations!

Chew and Chat

Some table manners have survived for centuries with good reason. Remind your kids:

·   Not to chew with their mouths open. No one wants to see what's in their mouths.

·   Not to talk while eating. Again, no one wants to see what's in their mouths.

·   If they need to remove something from their mouth (such as a pit or a bone), remove it the same way they ate it. If they ate fish from a fork and discovered a bone, have them remove it with their fork...

No matter how crazy mealtime can get in your house, a few basic table manners will serve you (and your kids!) well. Find out which rules work for you, and which you are willing to bend every now and then.

Sources and Exam Questions

Text C is a letter written in 1819 by Lord Byron, to a woman he was in love with.

Text D is a letter written in 1972 by an engineer working in Saudi Arabia to his wife.

2. With reference to both texts, write about what they show about the development of language over time.

[48 marks]

Text C — a letter to the Countess Teresa Guiccioli (1819), by Lord Byron

My dearest Teresa-

I have read this book in your garden; - my love, you were absent, or else I could not have read it. It is a favorite book of yours, and the writer was a friend of mine. You will not understand these English words, and *others* will not understand them, - which is the reason I have not scrawled them in Italian. But you will recognize the handwriting of him who passionately loves you, and you will divine that, over a book which was yours, he could only think of love. In that word, beautiful in all languages, but most so in yours - *Amor mio* - is comprised my existence here and hereafter. I feel I exist here, and I fear that I shall exist hereafter, - as to *what* purpose you will decide; my destiny rests with you, and you are a woman, seventeen years of age, and two out of a convent. I wish that you had stayed there, with all my heart, - or, at least, that I had never met you in your married state.

But all this is too late. I love you, and you love me, - at least, you *say so*, and *act* as if you *did* so, which last is a great consolation in all events. But I more than love you, and cannot cease to love you.

Think of me, sometimes, when the Alps and the ocean divide us, - but they never will, unless you *wish* it.

B.

Text D — a letter written from a husband to his wife (1972)

Dearest Julia,

    I arrived here in Riyadh on Monday evening after the most awful flight. I should be feeling really happy and excited, I suppose, but I am already missing you. Back in England, the thought of being separated from you for three months didn't seem so bad but now just the thought of being without you *even for a week* makes me feel desolate.

I suppose I'm just feeling a bit homesick, jetlagged and, dare I admit it, even a bit lonely. Yes, that's *me* talking, the person who always says he likes his own company!

I've met a few people so far and they seem really nice. I start work tomorrow – Saturday – so I expect that I won't feel so bad once I get stuck in to things. All I know is that already I can't wait till March when I'll be back home with you in our nice little house that has a garden and trees and rain! Yes *rain*, can you believe it?

I know you'll be thinking I'm a terrible wimp but I do hope you're missing me the same. Give my love to all the family and tell them I'm fine (even though I'm not!).

Will write again soon.

All my love
Toby x

Attitudes Towards Language Change

If there's one subject that's likely to cause a row down at the annual linguists' convention then it's language change. More people have got more bees in more bonnets over this than anything else. Time to get stuck in...

Attitudes towards Language Change can be Prescriptivist or Descriptivist

There are **two** main approaches to language change:

Prescriptivism

1) Prescriptivism involves stating a **set** of **rules** that people should follow in order to use language '**properly**' (**prescribing** what the language **should be like**).

2) Prescriptivists believe that language should be **written** and **spoken** in a certain way — in English this means using **Standard English** and **RP** (see p. 27). Other **varieties** of English are seen as **incorrect** and **inferior**.

3) Prescriptivists argue that it's **essential** to stick to the rules of the **standard** form, so that everyone can **understand** each other.

4) The prescriptivist view is that language **decays** as it **changes**, and the only way to stop **standards falling** further is to try and **stop linguistic change**.

Descriptivism

1) Descriptivism involves **describing** how language is actually **used**.

2) Descriptivists **don't** say that aspects of language are '**correct**' or '**incorrect**'. They believe that different **varieties** of English should all be **valued equally**.

3) The idea is that language **change** is **inevitable**, so it's a **waste of time** to try and **stop** it. Instead, descriptivists record **how** and **why** change occurs, rather than assuming all change is bad.

4) Some descriptivists see **language change** as **progress** — they believe that English is becoming more **accurate** and **efficient**. E.g. they'd say that Old English inflections were lost because they no longer served a purpose.

5) Other descriptivists, like **David Crystal**, argue that language change is **neither** progress nor decay, as all languages **change** in **different** ways (e.g. some languages gain inflections).

Prescriptivist Attitudes have been around for a Long Time

1) In the second half of the eighteenth century there was a sudden flourishing of **grammar books** that outlined what the **rules** of grammar should be. The most influential was Robert Lowth's ***A Short Introduction to English Grammar (1762)***. He argued that some constructions were grammatically **wrong**, e.g. split infinitives:

> **THE SPLIT INFINITIVE**
> - The infinitive (*to + verb*) should not be split by an **adverb**. The most famous example is *to boldly go*, from *STAR TREK™*.
> - Lowth argued that the construction *to + verb* is a **complete grammatical unit** and that's how it should remain.
> - However, the **meaning** isn't affected whether you say *to boldly go* or *to go boldly*, so **descriptivists** would argue that it's a **pointless** rule.

He was going to split an awful lot more than an infinitive if he didn't get up quick-smart.

2) Other prescriptivist texts have been more flexible about certain grammar rules, e.g. Henry Fowler's ***A Dictionary of Modern English Usage (1926)***. Fowler argued against some of Lowth's rules, because he thought that constructions should be used if they **sounded comfortable**, e.g. ending a sentence with a preposition:

| Fowler would argue that: | *That depends on what they are hit <u>with</u>* |
| sounds much better than: | *That depends on <u>with</u> what they are hit* |

3) However, many people still argue that certain rules **shouldn't** be **broken**, even though they **don't** affect the **meaning** of a sentence. For example, people often complain about constructions like *different <u>to</u>* and *different <u>than</u>*. They claim it should be *different <u>from</u>* because that's what you'd say in **Latin**, even though it's not the way that most English speakers say it.

Attitudes Towards Language Change

Descriptivism has become much more Popular in Recent Times

1) *The Oxford English Dictionary* (OED) was first published in the early **20th century**.

2) The editors of the dictionary were **descriptivists** — they stated in the **preface** that their **aim** was to **record** the language as it was, **not** to **prescribe** rules. Lots of other modern dictionaries have the same aim.

3) However, most people look words up in the dictionary to **make sure** they get a **meaning** or spelling 'right'. This shows that most people think of dictionaries as **prescriptive rule books**, not just records of the language.

> Many linguists are completely **against** prescriptivism. In the 1980s **Milroy and Milroy** argued that language change is **inevitable** and shouldn't be fought against. They also argued **against** the **high status** of **Standard English**. They claimed that fears about **falling standards** meant that people are often **discriminated** against, e.g. by employers, if they **don't** follow the **arbitrary** rules that were set out by grammarians in the **18th century**.

4) However, **Cameron** (**1995**) argued that prescriptivism **shouldn't** be **discounted** as just people being **fussy** or **pedantic** about something that doesn't really matter.

5) She's a **descriptivist**, but argues that **prescriptivism** shows that people realise that **language** is an important **social tool** and **care** about how it's used.

6) She also argues that **fear** about **language change** often **symbolises** fear about **social problems** — people worry that **declining** standards of **language** mirror **declining** standards in **behaviour** and **education**.

7) This means that people **focus** on **language change** because they want to **make sense** of **bigger problems** in **society**. She argues that this should be used to **start** a **debate** about what **attitudes** towards language change **symbolise**, rather than just being discounted as an **illogical belief**.

There are Different ways to Study Language Change

These tips should be handy if you want to base your language investigation on language change.

You can use different **methodologies** to **study** language change. You could look at:

Lexis
New words are constantly being **added** to the language. You could focus on **borrowings** from **other languages** or the **impact** of **technology**. To do this you could look at the **etymology** (origin) of new words in the **OED**.

Grammar
For example, you could look at how **syntax** has become a lot **less complex** since the **19th century**. You could do this by **comparing** the syntax in a page of a **Dickens novel** with the syntax in a page of a **contemporary** one.

Phonology
For example, you could analyse how **accents** have **changed** in **broadcasting** by looking at how **newsreaders** spoke in the **1950s** compared to **today**. You could **transcribe** recordings from the different periods and **analyse** how their **pronunciation** has changed, using the **phonetic alphabet** (see p. 64).

Practice Questions

Q1 What is the difference between the prescriptive and descriptive approaches to language change?

Q2 What was the purpose of 18th century grammar books and dictionaries?

Q3 Outline one method you could use to study language change.

Essay Question

Q1 "Something must be done to halt the rapid decline in standards of English."

How far do you agree with this statement? Refer to prescriptivist and descriptivist views in your answer.

Some of these prescriptivists have got a real attitude problem...

...I mean, really, fancy telling people that the way they use language is wrong. Except, of course, everyone does it all the time. So maybe we're all prescriptivists at heart... Anyway, enough thinking, just try and force this into your brain — prescriptivism lays down rules about how the language should be, and descriptivism describes how it actually is. The clue's in the name really.

Attitudes Towards Language Variation

The thing you have to remember about English is that everyone who speaks it seems to have an opinion about it. Fortunately a lot of people have quite similar opinions, otherwise you'd be in for a very long night...

People have **Different Attitudes** towards **Standard English**

1) As one variety of the language became standardised (see p. 30-31), other varieties became seen as **less prestigious**.

2) **Standard English** is a **social dialect**. It's usually associated with **educated**, **middle** and **upper class** people. It's the way that you're taught to use English at school, and the language of **formal speech** and **writing**.

3) **Regional dialects** were associated with the **uneducated** and the **lower classes**, so it was seen as important to be able to use English '**properly**' if you wanted to be successful.

> - Prescriptivists see **Standard English** as the '**correct**' or '**pure**' form of the language.
> - Other varieties are sometimes thought to be '**corruptions**' of it.
> - There's a view that if you use another dialect, you're not using English '**properly**'.

> - However, **descriptivists** argue that all varieties of English should be **valued equally**.
> - There's **no reason** why Standard English should be seen as better than any other dialect.
> - They claim that people shouldn't be considered **uneducated** if they **don't** use Standard English.

4) Whether it's **appropriate** to use Standard English depends on the **mode** and **context**. You'd expect a **formal text** to be **written** in Standard English, but you wouldn't necessarily expect people in an **informal** setting to **speak** to each other using Standard English.

People Have **Different Attitudes** towards **Accents** and **Dialects**

Someone's **accent** or **dialect** is often a good indication of **where they're from**. But it can also influence attitudes about a speaker's **social background** and **education**.

1) Some people **assume** that people who use **regional dialects** are **poorly educated** or **lower class**.

2) On the other hand, **regional varieties** of English are often associated with being **down-to-earth** and **modest**, e.g. because regional accents are seen as being more **accessible** to audiences, they are used more in voice overs in adverts (to **sell things**) and by presenters (on **national** as well as **local** radio or television stations).

> 1) **Workman (2008)** studied people's **perceptions** of different **accents**. Participants listened to recordings of different accents while they looked at photos of people.
>
> 2) It was found that participants rated the **intelligence** of the people in the photos differently, depending on which accent they thought they had.
>
> 3) **Yorkshire** accents were rated as sounding the **most intelligent**. When a recording of a **Birmingham** accent was played, the people in the photos were rated as being much **less intelligent**. Obviously this **isn't** actually **true**, but it shows how strong the **stereotypes** about different accents can be.

People have **Different Attitudes** towards **Slang**

Slang is sometimes seen as **low level**, **vulgar** language, which shouldn't be used in **writing** or in **formal situations**.

1) Some people think that if you use slang you're **undermining standards** by not using the language '**properly**'. They assume that people who use lots of slang are lower class and uneducated.

2) Slang is seen as the language of **informal speech**, so it's considered **inappropriate** to use it in a **formal context**, e.g. you'd lose marks if you wrote an essay using slang words and phrases.

3) This is because slang has a reputation for being **rebellious** and **subversive**, so it isn't formally accepted as a variety of English. Some people worry that it doesn't follow the 'proper' **spelling** and **grammar rules** of **Standard English**.

4) However, most slang words and phrases **do** follow the rules of Standard English — they're just more flexible.

5) People who are interested in slang argue that it's an **intelligent** and **creative** variety of language, which **changes** and **develops** very quickly. It also serves an important purpose in **social contexts** — people use it to **identify** themselves as part of a **group**.

Attitudes Towards Language Variation

There's **Debate** about **Regional Varieties** and **Slang** in **Education**

People have different attitudes towards the role of **standard** and **vernacular** varieties of English in education.

1) Linguists like **Milroy and Milroy** (1985) have argued that it's **not fair** to correct children for using **non-standard** varieties of English.

2) Children who use regional varieties of English can end up **struggling** at **school** because **Standard English** is **unfamiliar** to them. Because regional dialects are linked to **social class**, it's often **working class** children who are put at an immediate **disadvantage** because they're told that the language they use is **wrong**.

3) The Milroys argued that all varieties of English should be **valued equally** and children **shouldn't** be **discouraged** from using non-standard English.

"Henry VIII were a proper mardy bum..."

1) However, people such as **John Honey** (1997) argue that children **should** be taught **Standard English** at school, because this is the only way to make sure that all children have **equal opportunities**.

2) Because Standard English is the **prestigious** form of the language, children will be **disadvantaged** if they **don't** learn how to use it.

3) For example, they might miss out on **job opportunities** because they fill in applications using non-standard spelling. Employers might assume that they're unintelligent, and not give them the job. Therefore, it's important to teach all children the **writing skills** they need to succeed.

4) This viewpoint sees non-standard varieties as **barriers** to **universal communication**. Non-standard varieties are appropriate for informal speech, but **Standard English** should always be **favoured** because it ensures that **everyone** will be able to **understand** each other. This is called **bidialectism** — children end up using **two dialects**.

There are **Different** Ways to **Study Language Variation**

These tips should be handy if you want to base your language investigation on variation.

Different **methodologies** are used to **study** language variation, depending on the linguistic features you're focusing on:

Lexis
For example, you could look at poetry written in **dialects** and focus on **regional vocabulary**. You could also record **informal speech** and look at the amount of **slang** used by people of different ages.

Phonology
Phonemic transcriptions (p.64) from recordings of people with different **accents** are the best way to study different phonological features. They are compared and contrasted, highlighting **distinctive features** in particular accents.

Grammar
For example, researchers might compare transcriptions of the speech of a **Standard English** speaker with someone with a **regional dialect**. A good place to start looking is the **verb forms**, e.g. whether a speaker says *the dog wants fed* or *the dog wants feeding*.

Practice Questions

Q1 Name a mode and context that the use of Standard English might be associated with.

Q2 Outline the negative associations that some people might have with regional varieties of English.

Q3 Outline the two different viewpoints on the use of slang.

Q4 What did Milroy and Milroy argue about the role of Standard English in education?

Q5 Why do some people feel that it would be unfair not to teach children how to use Standard English?

Essay Question

Q1 Discuss whether non-standard varieties of English should have the same status as Standard English.

Never make up your mind about someone based on their accent...

Those poor Brummies, always getting a hard time about their accent. Personally, I think it's a lovely accent — and it doesn't seem to have done Cat Deeley's career any harm, or Jasper Carrott's, or Adrian Chiles'... Anyway, you need to know what other people think about language variation, whether you agree with them or think it's a load of twaddle.

Writing About Language Issues

'Writing about language issues' can sound tricky, but it doesn't have to be. It's really just about looking at how people feel about language, how important it is in society, and how it's symbolic for lots of other things. See — easy...

Language Issues aren't only for Linguists

1) Language issues are **frequently debated** in wider society.

2) Regional and national **media** — TV, radio, newspapers, magazines and the Internet — often conduct debates about the 'state of language' today. They discuss how it's **developing** and **changing** (for better or for worse).

3) Debates amongst linguists are sometimes brought to the **general public's attention** in this way.

4) While you might think that not many people are that bothered about how they and others **speak** or **write**, lots of non-specialist readers and writers care about **how** language is used. They think it reflects on the **individual** and on **society** as a whole, and they care **strongly enough** to join in the debate with their **own thoughts** or **examples**.

Some people complain that Language is Declining

Editorials in newspapers and magazines often have their say about the **state of language** today. They often link changes in language to a sense of **decline** rather than **development**. Some also link what they see as the deterioration of language with the **state of society** in general.

1) Writing for a non-specialist audience means writers can get their point across in lots of different ways.

2) If you look at how these texts work according to **linguistic frameworks**, you'll have a better understanding of how to put one together **yourself**. This sample magazine editorial is about **language change**:

> "It's apparent that the English language in its purest form, having enriched itself with borrowings and loans from the world's most progressive and intellectual cultures, has peaked. Worst of all, and to our horror, it is now receding. From the summits of Johnson and Lowth, English has tumbled almost toward the Neanderthal — a series of (albeit now electronic) monosyllabic grunts and minimalisms that reek of laziness rather than meaningful or worthy contributions to a formerly rich tapestry. The biggest culprit — "text message speak", has no place in linguistic debate, unless we realise that *pmsl* means not so much *piss myself laughing* as *please murder some language*."

Semantics

- The author specifically aims to create a **pessimistic atmosphere** by using terms with very **negative associations** like *receding, tumbled, horror, reek, laziness, culprit, murder.*

- The author also **juxtaposes** an idealised form of English (*peaked*, Johnson's and Lowth's *summits*), with a **physical fall** or **collapse** (*tumbled*), and a **lack of civilisation** (*Neanderthal*).

- Constructing a **different meaning** to *pmsl* also aims to make fun of the number of abbreviations that are used in informal English but maintains a serious undertone by using the term *murder*. The author's aim is to make the readers feel as if the English language is in **danger**, and it's their **responsibility** to stop the changes.

Grammar

- **Superlative adjectives** like *biggest, purest, most progressive* and *worst* give the text an air of **authority** and make it (both the text and the situation of English) seem much more **serious**.

- **Declarative sentences** e.g. *It's apparent that the English language... has peaked* also make the writing sound **authoritative** and mean that the points made in the text seem **definite** and **unquestionable**.

- Using **collective address** e.g. *unless we realise* directly **involves** the reader in taking responsibility for the problems the author identifies.

Lexis

- The lexis is mostly **non-specialist terminology** — the author doesn't use any linguistic phrases, and even **sensationalises** the writing by describing current English as *Neanderthal* and **exaggerating** everyone's emails and text messages into *grunts and minimalisms*.

- The lexis creates **oppositions** between the *meaningful* and *worthy... rich tapestry* of English *in its purest form*, and **informal varieties** of English, using *culprit* and *murder* to highlight the author's judgement that non-standard English like the kind used in text messages has *no place in linguistic debate*.

Writing About Language Issues

Some writers Embrace Language Change

Not everyone has the same feelings about language issues. Writing about something you support or agree with sometimes requires a **different approach** from when you're criticising or complaining.

> "If English had been to school it would've been the small kid in first year that matured into the playground bully — always pushing French in puddles and stealing Latin's dinner money. But it is dismissive of teachers' discipline, and has never been fully tamed by its many adoring students. The English language is a living organism, assuming myriad forms, rebuffing invasions (both military and prescriptive), constantly changing and developing. It is at once beyond control and our one pervasive constant — our identity. Shouldn't we be celebrating it for the unique world force it has now become?"

The **tone** and **style** of this piece of writing are different from the one on p. 42, because of the following techniques:

Personification

Writing that aims to highlight the good things about language change and variation often tries to give English a **personality** and make it appear **alive**. The aim is to make the reader feel like the language can't be **controlled** by prescriptivism, and that is exactly what makes it so great. Attributing the **qualities** needed to *rebuff* invasions also makes English seem **superior** to other languages.

Metaphor

The author places the concept of a 'living' English language into a **familiar human situation** — using a humorous metaphor of a school playground. This communicates the writer's message in a way that **non-specialists** can easily understand.

Rhetorical Questions

The rhetorical question at the end **leads** the reader into **agreeing** with the writer's opinion, by suggesting that there is no other possible logical answer.

Non-specialist Books on Language are Popular

Non-linguists are now quite **well informed** about language. This has resulted in lots of different opinions — everyone's got their **own view** on what constitutes 'good' or 'bad' English and whether they accept or understand certain phrases.

1) It's not only **textbooks** that discuss the various aspects of English.
2) **Linguists** write non-specialist titles, like David Crystal's *By Hook or by Crook: A Journey in Search of English* (2007) and *Txting: The Gr8 Db8* (2008), which are both very descriptive.
3) There are also books like the *How to talk proper in Liverpool: Lern Yersel' Scouse* or *Larn Yersel' Geordie* series, which are examples of **light-hearted** popular titles that document **regional variations**. There are also plenty of books about the differences between men and women in terms of **language and gender** too.
4) **Journalists / broadcasters** — who aren't necessarily experts on linguistics — sometimes write about language too, for example Melvyn Bragg's *The Adventure of English* (2003).

Practice Questions

Q1 How does the general public become involved in debates about language change?
Q2 What devices could be used to make ideas about language accessible to a non-specialist reader?
Q3 Apart from textbooks or revision guides, what sort of texts about English are available to a non-specialist reader?

Essay Question

Q1 Discuss the different styles you could adopt to get your views about English language across to a reader in a persuasive article.

Writing about language issues can give you writing about language issues...

My problem with it is the sheer wastefulness of the operation. It seems such a shame to use up so many precious words just writing about other words. They should be out there living the dream in marriage proposals, song lyrics and great political speeches, not cooped up in stuffy essays and newspaper articles. They'll probably run out one day, then we'll be sorry.

Sources and Exam Questions

Here are some exam-style questions, with sources like the ones you'll get in the real paper.

Text A is from the Preface to Samuel Johnson's *A Dictionary of the English Language* (1755).
Text B is from the linguist Jean Aitchison's book *The language web* (1997).

1. Comment on Johnson's and Aitchison's ideas using information from your language change studies.
   Discuss the way these two texts use language to communicate their ideas about language change.

[48 marks]

Text A — from the Preface to *A Dictionary of the English Language* (1755), by Samuel Johnson

I have, notwithstanding this discouragement, attempted a dictionary of the *English* language, which, while it was employed in the cultivation of every species of literature, has itself been hitherto neglected, suffered to spread, under the direction of chance, into wild exuberance, resigned to the tyranny of time and fashion, and exposed to the corruptions of ignorance, and caprices of innovation.

When I took the first survey of my undertaking, I found our speech copious without order, and energetick without rules: wherever I turned my view, there was perplexity to be disentangled, and confusion to be regulated; choice was to be made out of boundless variety, without any established principle of selection; adulterations were to be detected, without a settled test of purity; and modes of expression to be rejected or received, without the suffrages of any writers of classical reputation or acknowledged authority.

Having therefore no assistance but from general grammar, I applied myself to the perusal of our writers; and noting whatever might be of use to ascertain or illustrate any word or phrase, accumulated in time the materials of a dictionary, which, by degrees, I reduced to method, establishing to myself, in the progress of the work, such rules as experience and analogy suggested to me; experience, which practice and observation were continually increasing; and analogy, which, though in some words obscure, was evident in others.

In adjusting the ORTHOGRAPHY, which has been to this time unsettled and fortuitous, I found it necessary to distinguish those irregularities that are inherent in our tongue, and perhaps coeval with it, from others which the ignorance or negligence of later writers has produced. Every language has its anomalies, which, though inconvenient, and in themselves once unnecessary, must be tolerated among the imperfections of human things, and which require only to be registered; that they may not be increased, and ascertained, that they may not be confounded: but every language has likewise its improprieties and absurdities, which it is the duty of the lexicographer to correct or proscribe.

As language was at its beginning merely oral, all words of necessary or common use were spoken before they were written; and while they were unfixed by any visible signs, must have been spoken with great diversity, as we now observe those who cannot read catch sounds imperfectly, and utter them negligently. When this wild and barbarous jargon was first reduced to an alphabet, every penman endeavoured to express, as he could, the sounds which he was accustomed to pronounce or to receive, and vitiated in writing such words as were already vitiated in speech.

exuberance — unrestrained enthusiasm
caprice — unpredictable action, whim
fortuitous — happening by chance
coeval — contemporary, happening at the same time
vitiated — corrupted

Sources and Exam Questions

Text B — from *The language web* (1997), by Jean Aitchison

Naturally, language changes all the time. This is a fact of life. In the fourteenth century, Geoffrey Chaucer noted that *in forme of speche is chaunge* 'language changes' (see figure I.I), and the same is true today. But change is one thing. Decay is another. Is our language really changing for the worse, as some people argue?

Of course not. Over a hundred years ago, linguists — those who work on linguistics, the study of language — realised that different styles of language suit different occasions, but that no part of language is ever deformed or bad. People who dispute this are like cranks who argue that the world is flat. Yet flat-earth views about language are still widespread. As the Swiss linguist Ferdinand de Saussure said over seventy-five years ago: 'No other subject has spawned more absurd ideas, more prejudices, more illusions or more myths.' Things have not changed very much since then.

On inspection, the web of worries surrounding change turns out to be largely traditional, somewhat like the worries each new generation of parents has about its offspring. Laments about language go back for centuries.

A fourteenth-century monk complained that the English practise *strange wlaffyng, chytering, harryng, and garryng grisbittyng* 'strange stammering, chattering, snarling and grating tooth-gnashing'. And the complaints continued. 'Tongues, like governments, have a natural tendency to degeneration', wrote the lexicographer Samuel Johnson, in the preface to his famous *Dictionary of the English language* published in 1755.

Eighteenth-century worries are perhaps understandable. Around 1700, the seemingly fixed grammar of Latin aroused great admiration, at a time when English itself was in a fairly fluid state. Many people hoped to lay down similar firm precepts for English, and assumed that somebody, somewhere, knew what 'correct English' was. Jonathan Swift wrote a famous letter to the Lord Treasurer in 1712 urging the formation of an academy to regulate language use. He complained that 'many gross improprieties' could be found in the language of 'even the best authors'. But 'correct English' was as hard to define then as it is now. In practice upper- and middle-class speech was often praised as 'good', artificially supplemented by precepts from logic and imitations of various Latin usages.

Language Frameworks

You should be familiar with this stuff from AS, but for A2 you need to be really confident that you understand technical terms and can use them in your analysis. So it's probably worth a quick recap I'd say...

You should aim to Analyse all Texts in a Similar way

If you have to analyse a piece of language or discourse, there are several things to think about:

1) **Genre** — **what kind** of language it is. Written discourses could be **instruction booklets** or **adverts**, and spoken discourses could be **formal speeches** to an audience or **casual conversations** between friends.

2) **Register** — a type of language that's appropriate for a particular audience or situation, e.g. the language of a political party or the language of the justice system. Register also includes the level of **formality** in a discourse.

3) **Audience** — the **listener** or **reader**. When you're analysing language, think about how the audience is **addressed**. It might be **formal** or **informal**, **direct** or **indirect**. For example, in advertising the audience is often directly addressed as *you*.

4) **Subject** — what the discourse is **about**. This will be reflected in the **lexical choices**, e.g. a discussion about healthy eating may contain words like *low-fat*, *diet*, and *nutrition*.

5) **Purpose** — what the speaker or writer is trying to **achieve** through language (e.g. to persuade, instruct, etc.).

6) **Mode** — whether the language is **written or spoken**. You can also get **mixed modes** — e.g. in text messages, where the language is written, but contains many of the informal features of spoken language.

There are Seven Main Language Frameworks

This table is an **overview** of what makes up each language framework (also called **linguistic frameworks**, or **toolkits**) and how they can be used. You should use this every time you **analyse** a text.

Lexis	• **Lexis** means the **vocabulary** of a language — the total stock of words. • When you're analysing spoken and written language you'll notice words that share a **similar topic** or **focus**. For example, in an advert for mobile phones you'd find words such as *SMS*, *text-messaging*, and *battery life*. Words that are linked together in this way are known as a **lexical field**.
Semantics	• **Semantics** is the study of how **meaning** is created through words and phrases. Sometimes this meaning is **explicit**, but sometimes it's **implicit**. A word will have a **literal** meaning but it can also be **associated** with other meanings. • For example, the word *red* refers to a **colour**, but it can also be associated with **danger**.
Grammar	• **Grammar** is the system of **rules** that governs how words and sentences are **constructed**. There are three parts to this: 1) A system that **groups** words into classes according to their **function** (e.g. nouns or verbs). 2) A system of **rules** about how these types of words function in relation to each other (**syntax**). 3) The individual units that make up whole words (**morphology**).
Phonology	• **Phonology** is the study of **sounds** in English — how they're **produced** and how they're **combined** to make words. • This framework includes **Non-Verbal Aspects of Speech** (NVAS) or **prosody** — features of spoken language such as pace, stress, rhythm and intonation.
Pragmatics	• **Pragmatics** is sometimes called **language in use**. It's about how social conventions, context, personality and relationships influence the **choices** people make about their language. • For example, how you address other people shows **levels of formality** and **social conventions** — a student might address a teacher as *Miss Rogers* or *Lizzie* depending on what the college or school expects, and what the teacher finds acceptable.
Graphology	• **Graphology** is the study of the **appearance** of the writing and the effect this has on a text. • When you discuss a text's graphology you describe and analyse features like the **typeface**, the **positioning** of text on a page and the relationships between **text** and **images**.
Discourse	• **Discourse** is an **extended** piece of spoken or written language, made up of more than one **utterance** (in spoken language), or more than one **sentence** (in written language).

Language Frameworks

Discourse has a Structure

The way language is organised is called its **discourse structure**. You need to look out for different features, depending on whether the discourse is written or spoken.

1) In **written discourse**, look at how a text is **put together**. It may have an **opening** section which leads the reader into the text. The following sections may develop a **theme or argument**. The final section may make some kind of **conclusion**.

2) In **spoken discourse** the structure can be less organised. For example, **conversations** are often **unpredictable** and speakers often **digress** (go off the subject). This is because conversations are usually **spontaneous**.

3) Even spontaneous conversations have some structure, though.

There'll often be an **opening sequence**, e.g.

> Speaker 1: *Hi, how you doing?*
> Speaker 2: *Fine thanks. How about you?*

This is often followed by **turn-taking** as the speakers talk about a topic (or topics). There's often a **closing sequence** too, e.g.

> Speaker 1: *Well, nice seeing you...*
> Speaker 2: *You too.*
> Speaker 1: *Catch you later.*

4) You can also look at how the discourse **fits together** — **cohesion**. There are **two types** of cohesion — **lexical** and **grammatical**. One example of grammatical cohesion is using **adverbs** like *furthermore* and *similarly* at the beginning of a sentence or paragraph to link it to the previous one. Lexical cohesion is when the words in the discourse **relate** to each other throughout, e.g.

> *There was no sign of **the car** — **her lift** was obviously stuck in **traffic**. Was it really worth it, just for a **ride** in a **Porsche**?*

There are Three Main Steps to Discourse Analysis

1) The **first step** in **discourse analysis** is to think about **what kind** of discourse you are looking at. To do this you need to think about genre, register, audience, subject, purpose and mode.

2) The **next step** is to look at how each of the **language frameworks** contributes to the discourse. You might not need to use all of the language frameworks, or you might need to give more emphasis to one than another. It depends on the discourse.

3) And finally, don't forget to discuss **discourse structure** (how the text has been organised) and **cohesion** (the devices used to knit the text together).

Dr. B. Godwin. Harvard's leading phonologist.

Practice Questions

Q1 Name six things you should consider when analysing a piece of language.

Q2 What seven items can be found in a linguistic toolkit?

Q3 Define the term discourse.

Q4 Explain the key features in the structure of written and spoken discourse.

Q5 What is grammatical cohesion?

Q6 Outline the three main steps to discourse analysis.

My bike's fallen apart — I don't think the frame works...

This nuts and bolts stuff really isn't anything to get freaked out about. If you think about it, it's much easier to learn than all that other wishy washy waffly stuff, and the more you know the better you'll look in the exam. These pages are basically spewing potential marks left, right and centre, so you just need to drink up as much as possible. Sorry, that was gross...

Introduction to Grammar

You might not believe this, but some people think that grammar is really dull and boring, when actually... erm...

Grammar controls how Language is Constructed

1) Grammar is the set of **structural rules** that controls the way language works.
2) There are **three aspects** of grammar that you need to focus on — word classes, syntax and morphology.
3) **Word classes** define the **roles** that each word can play in a sentence. **Syntax** is the set of **rules** that control where each word class can appear in a sentence. **Morphology** describes the **construction** of individual words.

There are Eight Main Word Classes

Words are **categorised** by the **function** they have in a sentence.
There are eight main **word classes** — also called **parts of speech**.

Word Class	Function	Example
Nouns	'naming' words	*London, book, romance*
Adjectives	describe nouns (and sometimes pronouns)	*large, sunny, featureless*
Verbs	'doing' words	*jump, read, return*
Adverbs	describe verbs (and sometimes adjectives and other adverbs too)	*steadily, incredibly, sadly*
Pronouns	take the place of nouns	*you, they, him, me, it*
Conjunctions	'connecting' words	*and, or, but, because*
Prepositions	define relationships between words in terms of time, space and direction	*before, underneath, through*
Determiners	give specific kinds of information about a noun (e.g. quantity or possession)	*a, the, two, his, few, those*

Word Classes are Controlled by Rules

Word classes can take **different positions** in a sentence, but there are **grammatical rules** about how they work with each other (**syntax**). In the following sentence you can see all the word classes working together:

She	*saw*	*the*	*new*	*manager*	*and*	*his*	*assistant*
pronoun	verb	determiner	adjective	noun	conjunction	determiner	noun

at	*the*	*store*	*yesterday.*
preposition	determiner	noun	adverb

1) People **instinctively** know the rules for connecting words together. For example, you know that words in this order — *doctor she the yesterday saw* — are wrong, and you can **rearrange** them into something that makes sense straight away — *she saw the doctor yesterday*.
2) You also intuitively know **less obvious rules** about word order — you'd always say *the big brown bear* rather than *the brown big bear*, because you know that adjectives of size **come before** those of colour.
3) Sometimes there are **fewer restrictions** — some sentences mean the same thing wherever a word is placed, particularly with **adverbs**, e.g. *I **completely** disagree* or *I disagree **completely***.
4) Sometimes the **meaning** of a sentence changes depending on the position of a word:
   *He **quickly** told me to leave* (he said it fast) **or** *He told me to leave **quickly*** (he wanted me to leave fast)

Grammatical rules Affect Word Formation

Grammar affects word formation (morphology) because extra bits have to be added to words to **change** things like number or tense. The extra bits are called **inflections**. Here are a couple of examples.

• *-s* is added to *cup* to change a **singular** noun into a **plural** — *cups* (see p. 50).
• *-ed* is added to *remember* to change the **present** tense verb into the **past** tense *remembered* (see p. 52).

Introduction to Grammar

Grammar Choices can Influence the reader or listener

You can influence your **audience** in different ways by **changing** the **grammar** of a word or sentence.

Tense

1) Events that happened in the past are usually described in the past tense. Sometimes however, in both spoken and written discourse, past events are described using **present tense forms**.

> • *So she **went** up to the customer and **gave** him a good telling off.* ← past tense
> • *So she **goes** up to the customer and **gives** him a good telling off.* ← present tense

2) The first example sentence is in the past tense. There is a clear sense that some **time has passed** since the event actually happened. In the second, although the action happened in the past, the present tense creates a more **immediate** and **dramatic** impact. You'll see this technique used a lot in **newspaper headlines**:

> **New evidence casts doubt on verdict**   **Pop star admits to private hell**   **Cop raid closes nightclub**

Plurals

1) As well as telling you that there's more than one of something, plurals can **increase** the scale of a **scene**.

> • *There was a **mass** of fans outside the hotel.* ← singular
> • *There were **masses** of fans outside the hotel.* ← plural

2) Using the singular form *mass* creates the impression of a **specific** body of people. Adding the **-es** inflection to form the plural *masses* creates the image of a **big crowd** of people across a **wider area**.

Adjectives

1) Adjectives are a great way to **influence** your **audience** — compare the following two examples:

> • *If you're looking for the holiday of a lifetime, simply treat yourself to a **great** resort in Sri Lanka. Relax in **fine** accommodation.* ← simple adjectives
> • *Looking for the holiday of a lifetime? Simply treat yourself to the **greatest** resort in Sri Lanka. Relax in the **finest** accommodation.* ← superlative adjectives

2) These are similar **advertising discourses**, but the second example is much more **persuasive** than the first. The writer uses **superlative** adjectives (see p. 51) (*greatest* and *finest*) rather than the simple adjectives in the first example (*great* and *fine*).

3) There are some **other grammatical features** that influence the reader in these examples.

   • The second example begins with a **question**. This makes the reader feel **involved immediately**.

   • The first example uses the **indefinite article** *a* before the adjective *great*, but the second uses the **definite article** *the* before *greatest* (see p. 54). This makes the reference very **specific** in the second example (it is **the** greatest resort), but the first could be referring to any one of **several** resorts.

Practice Questions

Q1   Define the terms word class, syntax and morphology.

Q2   What function do conjunctions have in a sentence?

Q3   What function do prepositions have in a sentence?

Q4   Identify each word according to word class in the following sentence:
There were few talented actors in town, but the agent from Paris skilfully located the star he needed.

Q5   Give two examples of an inflection.

Q6   What effect can the use of superlative adjectives create?

My grammar's brilliant — she always gives me 20 quid at Christmas...

Grammar was clearly invented by authoritarian loons — look how many times you see the words 'rules' and 'control'. If you don't like being put in a box and held back by 'the man', then it's time to go and live in a commune in Holland and rename yourself Sage. If, however, you want to pass your Eng Lang exam, then you'll have to put up with it for a teensy bit longer.

Nouns and Adjectives

Noun pay attention (ho ho ho), because *noun's* the time (tee hee hee) to learn about... err... nouns. And also adjectives... The first thing you need to remember is that nouns are naming words, and adjectives are describing words.

Nouns can be **Divided** into **Categories**

There are different **types** of nouns. They can refer to unique **people** or **places** (**proper nouns**), or identify more general **objects**, **states** or **groups** (**common nouns**). See below for some examples.

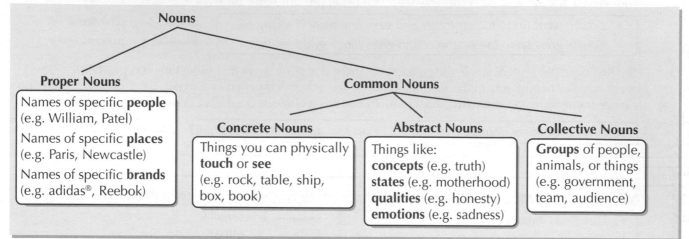

Nouns can be either **Singular** or **Plural**

1) To form the **plural** of a noun you usually add an *-s* or *-es* so that you get, for example, *birds,* or *bus**es***.

2) Where a noun ends in a consonant and then *-y*, the *-y* is replaced with *-ies* e.g. *lady* ⟶ *lad**ies***.

3) Word endings that include an *f* like *knife* and *dwarf* often replace the *f* with *-ves* ⟶ *kni**ves*** and *dwar**ves***.

4) Some nouns form **irregular plurals**, different from the **standard** pattern, e.g.
woman ⟶ *women*　　*foot* ⟶ *feet*　　*mouse* ⟶ *mice*

5) There are some nouns that **don't change their form** at all, whether they are singular or plural, e.g. *deer* and *sheep* stay the same even when you are referring to more than one.

Nouns can be classified as **Count Nouns** or **Mass Nouns**

1) **Count nouns** (a bit obviously) can be **counted** — like *brick*. You can have *one brick, two bricks, three bricks,* and so on. Nouns that form irregular plurals can be count nouns too — *one mouse, two mice,* etc.

2) **Mass nouns** can't be counted. Nouns like these **don't** have a **plural**, e.g. you talk about *information* rather than *informations*.

3) Some nouns can function as **both** count and mass nouns, depending on the **context**. For example, in the phrase *war is evil, war* is a **mass noun** — it refers to war in general. However, *war* becomes a **count noun** when you use a determiner — e.g. *the war is evil.* This time *war* refers to a **specific** war rather than war in general.

Nouns can be **Modified** to give **More Information**

Nouns **don't usually stand alone**. They're often accompanied by words that **modify** them or that tell you **more** about them. There are two types of modifier — **pre-modifiers** and **post-modifiers**.

- **Pre-modifiers** — these come **before** the noun, e.g. a sign that reads *Dangerous Animal*. The adjective *dangerous* premodifies *animal* and tells you something about it. You can also have **more than one** pre-modifier, e.g. *very dangerous animal* — *very* and *dangerous* are both pre-modifiers.

- **Post-modifiers** — these come after the noun, e.g. *Examination in progress*. The noun *examination* is postmodified by *in progress* — it tells the reader something about the examination.

In **noun phrases**, the noun is called the **head word** — the most important word of the phrase. The other words **modify** it.

determiner	pre-modifier	head word	post-modifier
the	*largest*	*whale*	*in the world*

Nouns and Adjectives

Adjectives **Describe Nouns**

Adjectives are classified according to their **position** — **before** or **after** the noun.

1) **Attributive** adjectives are **premodifying**, e.g. *the **sudden** noise*, or *the **red** balloon*.

2) **Predicative** adjectives are **postmodifying**. They're usually **linked** to the noun they are modifying by a form of the verb *be*:

> **Examples of predicative adjectives**
>
> - *Revision is **brilliant*** — the adjective is **linked** to the noun by a form of the verb *be*.
> - *The food looked **amazing*** — although forms of *be* are the most common links, **other verbs** can link the adjective to the noun (e.g. *looked, seemed, felt*).

Adjectives also make **Comparisons**

Adjectives are **gradable** — they can show **how much** of a certain property a noun displays.

1) **Comparative adjectives** are generally formed by adding an *-er* **inflection**. For example, the simple adjective *long* becomes the comparative adjective *long**er***.

2) **Superlative adjectives** are generally formed by adding *-est*. For example, *long* becomes the superlative *long**est***.

> Look back at p. 49 to see the effects of gradable adjectives in the holiday advertisement texts. Gradable adjectives make you interpret the sentences and the type of accommodation they advertise differently:
>
>
>
> | *fine* accommodation | *finer* accommodation | *finest* accommodation |
> |:---:|:---:|:---:|
> | **simple adjective** | **comparative adjective** | **superlative adjective** |

3) Some adjectives are **irregular** in the way they form comparatives and superlatives:

Adjective	Comparative	Superlative
good	→ better	→ best
bad	→ worse	→ worst
much	→ more	→ most

4) Some adjectives need *more* and *most* to form comparisons. For example, you can't say *significanter* or *significantest*. You use ***more** significant* or ***most** significant* to make the comparison.

Practice Questions

Q1 Name the three types of common nouns and give an example of each.

Q2 What's the difference between mass nouns and count nouns?

Q3 What is a post-modifier of a noun?

Q4 What's the difference between attributive and predicative adjectives?

Q5 Give the comparative and superlative forms of the following adjectives:
big, pretty, convincing, bad, colourful, clean.

Road, pavement, car park — all concrete nouns...

I think it's disgraceful that in the 21st century we're still calling some nouns 'common'. How exactly are they expected to ever have equal chances in life if they're stuck with this negative label? Especially when the 'proper' nouns have always looked down on them. It's discrimination at its worst — I really thought that an English Language book would have known better...

Verbs and Adverbs

Ok, try to get your head round this first — verbs are doing words, adverbs tell you how the doing is being done. Hmmm, no I'm none the wiser either. Read the rest of the page and see if it makes it any clearer, I'm off for a lie down...

Verbs tell you exactly **What Happens**

The base form of a verb is called the **infinitive** — it normally follows 'to', e.g. to *be*, to *laugh*, or to *think*. You can describe verbs in two ways:

1) **Main Verbs** (lexical verbs) identify the action of the sentence — e.g. *she sings like a hyena, he gave me his shoe.* The **verbs** *sing* and *gave* tell you what **action** is taking place.

2) **Auxiliary Verbs** go **before** the main verb in a sentence. They give **extra information** about the main verb and can affect the **meaning** of the sentence. There are **two** types of auxiliary verb:

Primary auxiliaries

There are three primary auxiliaries — *do, have,* and *be*.

- I **do** like you
- I **am** leaving tomorrow

Primary auxiliaries can also be **main verbs**:

- I **have** a surprise for you

Modal auxiliaries

Modal auxiliaries can **only** occur with reference to a main verb. For example:

can	*could*	*will*	*would*	*must*
may	*might*	*shall*	*should*	

- I **can** play the drums
- I **must** do something

Verbs can **Change** their endings depending on **Who** is **Doing** the **Action**

The **endings** of verbs can alter depending on **who** is doing the action — the **first**, **second** or **third person**.

Person	Singular Pronoun	Verb	Plural Pronoun	Verb
First	I	play	We	play
Second	You	play	You	play
Third	She/He/It	play**s**	They	play

Only the verb in the third person singular changes its ending — you add an -s to get plays. This rule applies to most of the verbs in English.

Changes to the ends of words that affect the grammar of the sentence are called **inflections**.

Verbs can tell you **When** something happens

Verbs change depending on whether something is happening in the **past**, **present** or **future**.

1) **Present tense** tells you about 'now' and uses the **base form** of the verb, e.g. *I write* or *they dance* — unless it's the third person singular (see above), when you need to add the *-s* **inflection**, e.g. *she/he/it talks*.

2) **Past tense** tells you about the past (obviously), e.g. *I danced yesterday*, or *He missed the bus*. For most verbs, you form the past tense by **adding -ed** on the end — another **inflection**.

3) **Future tense** — some people say that there's no future tense in English. This is because there **isn't** anything specific (like *-s*, or *-ed*) that you can **add** to a verb to show that the action will happen in the future. The future is expressed in **other ways** — often by using **modal auxiliary** verbs like **will** or **shall**.
   e.g. *I **shall** see you tomorrow.*   *I **will** pick you up at eight.*

4) You can also use the **present tense** to talk about **future events** — e.g. *Rachel is **playing** hockey on Saturday*.

Verbs **Don't** always change in the **Same Way**

1) Most verbs are **regular** — they follow the same patterns outlined above.

2) Some verbs are **irregular** — they don't change like you'd expect, e.g. *I drink* becomes *I **drank***, not *I **drinked***. Other verbs with irregular past tenses include **run**, **sing**, **write**, and **speak**.

3) The verb *be* is very irregular — the forms it can take are the infinitive *to be*, plus *am, are, is, was,* and *were*. It changes more than any other verb according to **person** (first, second or third), **number** and **tense**.

Verbs and Adverbs

Verbs can create an **Active** or **Passive** voice

Sentences that involve an **action** can focus on either the **subject** or the **object** (see p. 56 for more on this).

Active Voice

The **active voice** is when the **subject** is the focus and **performs** the action described by the verb, e.g:

- Ahmed **kicked** the ball.

The subject, *Ahmed*, acts **directly** upon the object — *the ball*. The object **receives** the action of the verb.

Passive Voice

The **passive voice** is less direct. It focuses on the **object**. The **order changes** so that the object comes first, followed by the subject, e.g:

- The ball **was kicked** by Ahmed.

The passive voice makes sentences seem more **formal**.

Verbs can change depending on the **Aspect**

Aspect shows whether the action described by the verb has **finished**, or is still **being performed**.

PROGRESSIVE ASPECT

1) The **progressive** (or **continuous**) aspect refers to actions that don't have a definite end.
2) It's made up of one of the auxiliary forms of *be* and the **present participle** of a verb, which is the **base form** + *-ing*.
3) For example, in the sentence *They **are doing** well*, *are* is an auxiliary form of *be* and *doing* is the present participle of *do*.

PERFECT ASPECT

1) The **perfect aspect** tells you about an action that has a definite end.
2) It's made up of one of the present forms of *have* (has/have) and the past tense form of the verb, e.g. *They **have bought** a car.*
3) The **past perfect** aspect is formed in the same way but with the past tense of *have* (had), e.g. *I **had missed** it.*

Adverbs are used to **Modify** verbs

Adverbs are mostly used to modify verbs, but they can modify nouns and adjectives too. Most people recognise adverbs as '**-ly** words' but many have different endings. Here are a **few ways** that adverbs **modify meaning**:

- Adverbs of **manner** — how something is done — e.g. *He talks **incessantly**.*
- Adverbs of **place** — where something is happening — e.g. *The book is **here**.*
- Adverbs of **time** — when something is happening — e.g. *The exam is **tomorrow**.*
- Adverbs of **duration** — how long something happens for — e.g. *The journey took **forever**.*
- Adverbs of **frequency** — how often something takes place — e.g. *Mandy visits **sometimes**.*
- Adverbs of **degree** — the extent to which something is done — e.g. *We **completely** understand.*

Some adverbs **express feelings** or opinions — ***Hopefully**, we'll find out where the garage is.*
Adverbs can also **link** sentences together — *The man was a great athlete. **However**, he didn't have a clue about adverbs.*

Practice Questions

Q1 Name the three primary auxiliary verbs.
Q2 What are inflections?
Q3 Give three examples of verbs with irregular past tenses.
Q4 What's the difference between the active voice and the passive voice? Give examples.
Q5 What's the difference between the progressive aspect and the perfect aspect? Give examples.
Q6 What is the function of adverbs?

All these verbs are making me feel a bit tense...

Verbs might seem dull, but they're actually really important. I mean, just think where we'd be without them — we wouldn't really be able to communicate at all. Or should I say, we not really at all. See what I mean? Anyway, everything on this page probably seems quite familiar, but make sure you go over it properly and learn the correct terms for everything.

Pronouns and Determiners

Pronouns, determiners, prepositions and conjunctions are little words, but that doesn't mean you can just ignore them. For a start that would be size discrimination, and anyway, they're pretty important, so it's probably best to learn them.

Pronouns *Take* the *Place* of *Nouns*

Pronouns are a **sub-class** of **nouns**. They can identify subjects and objects, just like nouns do.

1) **Personal** pronouns can replace people or things who are the **subject** of a sentence. They're classified in terms of **person** and are either **singular** or **plural**:

	Singular	Plural
First Person	I	we
Second Person	you	you
Third Person	he, she, it	they

e.g.   Sarah thanked Sanjay
↓
She thanked Sanjay
(3rd person singular subject pronoun)

2) Pronouns can also be used to replace the person or thing who is the **object** of the sentence:

	Singular	Plural
First Person	me	us
Second Person	you	you
Third Person	him, her, it	them

e.g.   Graham thanked Adam
↓
Graham thanked **him**
(3rd person singular object pronoun)

Pronouns are used in *Other Ways* too

1) **Interrogative** pronouns are used to **ask questions**. They are *which, what, who,* and *whose*. As with other pronouns, they help you **simplify** your sentences by **replacing nouns**, e.g:

- *Give me the name of **the person** you're looking for.* ⟶ **Who** *are you looking for?*
- *Tell me **the thing** you are going to do.* ⟶ **What** *are you going to do?*

2) These aren't the only words you use at the start of questions. *Why, where, how* and *when* are also interrogatives, but they are **adverbs**. Interrogative pronouns and adverbs are usually **classed together** as *wh-words*.

3) **Demonstrative** pronouns like *this, that, these* and *those* can **replace** people and things in a sentence where there's some **shared understanding** of what's being referred to, for example:

- If you're in the kitchen, you might ask *is this my coffee?* — only people who are also in the kitchen will be able to tell you.

- You use different demonstratives depending on the **distance** of the object from the speaker — *this* and *these* are objects **near** the speaker. You use *that* or *those* for objects **further away**.

Determiners show what the noun is *Referring To*

There are several determiners, which all **go before** the noun and show what it's referring to.

1) The **definite article** *the* and the **indefinite article** *a* refer to nouns. The definite article indicates something **specific**. The indefinite article indicates something more **general**, for example:

*Is that **the** frog?* (we are looking for, specifically) **or** *Is that **a** frog?* (or is it a toad?)

2) **Numerals** such as *one, two* and *three* (cardinal numbers) and *first, second* etc. (ordinal numbers) are determiners.

3) **Possessive determiners** like *my, your, his, her, its, our* and *their* are **possessive pronouns** used as determiners. They're used before a noun to show **possession**, e.g. ***my** car,* **his** *friend,* **their** *problem.*

4) **Quantifiers** are determiners that show **quantity**, like *few, many* and *enough*.

5) **Demonstrative adjectives**, e.g. *this, that, these,* and *those* are also determiners. They **look the same** as demonstrative pronouns but there is a **significant difference** between them. They refer to **specific** objects or people that the participants are **close to**, rather than replacing them like pronouns do:

*I like **those*** **or** *I like **those** shoes*
*(those **replaces** the noun — pronoun).*   *(those **precedes** the noun — adjective / determiner).*

Prepositions and Conjunctions

Prepositions show Relationships between things

Prepositions show the **relationship** between things in terms of **space**, **time** or **direction**. The preposition usually goes before the determiner and noun.

- The books are **underneath** the bed (spatial)
- He moved **towards** the door (directional)
- She left **before** the end (time)

Sometimes there's no determiner e.g. ➡
- See you **at** breaktime.
- We'll talk more about it **on** Friday.

Conjunctions are Linking Words

There are **two types** of conjunction — **coordinating** conjunctions and **subordinating** conjunctions.

1) **Coordinating conjunctions** are words like *and*, *but* and *or*. They **connect** single words or longer units of language (phrases and clauses) that have **equal status**:

| Robert **and** Bethany | A white shirt **or** a pink shirt | He kissed her on the cheek **and** she ran away |

The **coordinating conjunction** *and* connects the two names — neither is given more importance.

The **coordinating conjunction** *or* links two phrases.

The coordinating conjunction *and* links two **equal statements**.

2) **Subordinating conjunctions** are words like *since*, *although*, *because*, *unless*, *whether* and *whereas*. They link a main clause to one that's **less important** to the subject of the sentence:

| Some people find Maths really difficult, **whereas** others find it easy. |

There's more about clauses on p. 56-57.

The main clause is *Some people find Maths really difficult*. This is the main point of the sentence. The **subordinating conjunction** *whereas* introduces a less important clause *others find it easy*.

Subordinating conjunctions give **different meanings**. Some, like *after*, *before* and *until* are to do with **time**. Others, like *where* and *wherever* are about **place**.

1) Conjunctions are an important **cohesive device** — they help a discourse to flow smoothly.
2) A discourse **without** conjunctions seems very **disjointed** e.g. *Last night I went out. I bumped into my friend Hayley. We talked for a while. She had to leave early. She was babysitting for her auntie.*
3) If you add **conjunctions**, the discourse is much more **fluent** — e.g. *Last night I went out **and** I bumped into my friend Hayley. We talked for a while **but** she had to leave early **because** she was babysitting for her auntie.*

Practice Questions

Q1 What is the function of pronouns?
Q2 What's the difference between the pronouns *we* and *us*?
Q3 Name five types of determiners and give an example of each.
Q4 What do prepositions show? Give an example.
Q5 What are coordinating conjunctions? Give an example.
Q6 What are subordinating conjunctions? Give an example.

If pronouns take the place of nouns, what do protractors do?

Phew, there's lots to learn on these pages, but it's all useful stuff. The problem with all this is there are just so many terms to learn. But I'm afraid you're just going to have to keep reading these pages and testing yourself on them until you're sure you know your numerals from your quantifiers and your possessive pronouns from your demonstrative adjectives. Lucky you.

Phrases and Clauses

Sadly, this isn't a page full of useful phrases for when you go on holiday. So if you need to know how to ask the way to the bus station in Greek, or how to reserve a table in Japanese, I'm afraid you'll have to buy a different book.

Phrases are **Units** of **Language** that have a **Head Word**

Phrases are units of language built around a **head word** that identifies the type of phrase, e.g. in the noun phrase *the empty house*, the noun *house* is the head word. Basic sentences are created from a combination of phrases.

1) The simplest noun phrase (NP) possible is just a **noun itself**.
   It can be accompanied by a **pre-modifier**, a **post-modifier**, or both.

Pre-modifiers come before the noun. They're often a determiner, followed by an adjective.	Pre-modifiers		Head Word	Post-modifiers		Post-modifiers come after the noun.
	determiner	adjective	noun	preposition	noun	
	the	new	mayor	of	Bradford	

2) A very simple verb phrase (VP) has **one verb**, but you can also make up a verb phrase from the head word (a main verb) and one or more **auxiliary** verbs.

Auxiliary	Auxiliary	Head Word
should	have	passed

A **Clause** is a **Unit** of a **Sentence**

1) Sentences are made up of **clauses** — the **simplest meaningful units** of the sentence.

2) A **sentence** can be made up of **one clause** — e.g. *Katherine likes going walking*.

3) Or it can be made up of **more than one** clause. When there's more than one clause in a sentence, the clauses are usually separated by **conjunctions** — e.g. *Katherine likes going walking **but** she doesn't like running*.

4) **Clauses** can be made up of a **subject**, **verb**, **object**, **complement** and **adverbial**.

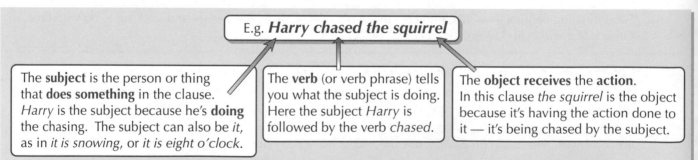

E.g. *Harry chased the squirrel*

The **subject** is the person or thing that **does something** in the clause. *Harry* is the subject because he's **doing** the chasing. The subject can also be *it*, as in *it is snowing*, or *it is eight o'clock*.

The **verb** (or verb phrase) tells you what the subject is doing. Here the subject *Harry* is followed by the verb *chased*.

The **object receives** the **action**. In this clause *the squirrel* is the object because it's having the action done to it — it's being chased by the subject.

A **complement** gives more **information about** the **subject** or **object**. It **completes** the **meaning** of the sentence it appears in, for example:

- In *Harry is a great guitarist*, the noun phrase (NP) *Harry* is the subject. The second NP in the sentence, *a great guitarist* is a **subject complement**. It **completes** the meaning of the sentence by giving information about the subject.

- In *Harry found the film appalling*, *Harry* is still the subject. But the adjective *appalling* refers to *the film*, which is the object, so *appalling* is the **object complement**.

An **adverbial** is a word or group of words that **refers back to the verb**. The simplest adverbial is just an adverb e.g. *Harry kicked the ball **quickly***. In *Harry is playing on Sunday*, the adverbial is *on Sunday* as it relates to the specific time that Harry will play. Adverbials usually describe **time**, **place** or **manner**.

5) The verb, complements and adverbials of a clause or sentence are sometimes also called the **predicate**.
   The term 'predicate' refers to any part of the clause that is **not the subject**, but that **modifies** it in some way.
   The verb is sometimes referred to as the **predicator**.

Phrases and Clauses

There are **Seven** Common Types of **Clause**

These are created by **different combinations** of subject (**S**), verb (**V**), object (**O**), complement (**C**) and adverbial (**A**):

S + V	Harry + played
S + V + O	Harry + played + a game
S + V + C	Harry + was + great
S + V + A	Harry + played + on Tuesday
S + V + O + O	Harry + gave + him + a drink
S + V + O + C	Harry + thought + his performance + disappointing
S + V + O + A	Harry + passed + the ball + quickly

Harry + was + great,
and boy did he know it.

Clauses are defined by **Status**

The **status** of a clause depends on its **constituents** and whether it can **stand alone** as a meaningful unit of language.

1) **Main clauses (independent clauses)** can stand alone and still make sense:

> Harry played.

2) **Coordinate clauses** occur in sentences where there are **two or more** independent clauses.
   - They're joined together by a **coordinating conjunction** like *and* or *but*. For example:

   > The band played for two hours **but** I had to leave early.

   - The clauses could **stand alone** and still **make sense** — *The band played for two hours. I had to leave early.*

3) **Subordinate clauses** can't stand alone. They have to be with a **main clause**.
   - A subordinate clause gives **extra information** about the main clause.
   - In most cases, a subordinate clause is led by a **subordinating conjunction** (like *since, although, because, unless, if, whether, while, whereas* etc.). This links it to the main clause. For example:

   main clause ➡️ | Will you pop in to see me **while** you're here tomorrow? | ⬅️ subordinate clause
   (the clause can't stand
   alone in a meaningful way)

   ⬆️ subordinating conjunction

4) **Combining clauses** — you can combine coordinate and subordinate clauses in the same sentence:

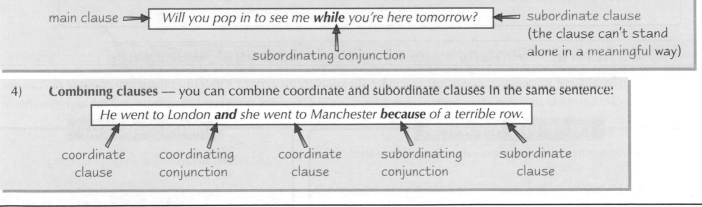

> He went to London **and** she went to Manchester **because** of a terrible row.

coordinate clause   coordinating conjunction   coordinate clause   subordinating conjunction   subordinate clause

Practice Questions

Q1 What is a head word?

Q2 What's the difference between a clause and a sentence?

Q3 What's the difference between a coordinate clause and a subordinate clause?

Q4 Identify the main clause and the subordinate clause in the following sentence:
    Can you get me some bread when you go to the shop?

Out of all the clauses, I'd say my favourite's Santa...

It's easy to get confused between phrases, clauses and sentences, but keep going over the differences between them until you feel like they could be your specialist subject on Mastermind (or at least in your A level English exam). Don't forget that a sentence can just be one clause, or a few clauses joined together with conjunctions.

Sentences

Sentences are pretty straightforward, but that doesn't mean that there's nothing to learn. In fact, there are loads of different types of sentence, and that means — yep, you've guessed it — loads more terms for you to learn. Hurray.

Sentences can be anything from very Simple to really Complex

There are **five** types of sentence — **minor**, **simple**, **compound**, **complex** and **compound-complex**.

1) **Minor sentences** are complete and meaningful statements that **don't have** a subject and verb combination. Lots of everyday sayings are minor sentences, e.g. *Be quiet. Goodbye. Sounds good.*

2) A **simple sentence** must have a **subject** and a **verb**. It should express a **complete thought**, e.g. *The snow falls.* *S*now is the **subject**, *falls* is the **verb**.

3) A **compound sentence** is an independent clause linked to another independent clause by a **coordinating conjunction**. Either one could be a main clause in a different sentence.

independent → *I went to Manchester **and** I went to Liverpool.* ← independent
clause   clause

coordinating conjunction

One too many clauses for Mr. Barrett.

4) A **complex sentence** consists of a main clause and a subordinate clause (or subordinating clauses). A **subordinating conjunction** connects the clauses together:

main clause → *The workers left the building **when** they heard.* ← subordinate clause

subordinating conjunction

5) A **compound-complex sentence** is made up of at least two **coordinate clauses** connected by a **coordinating conjunction**, and **at least one** subordinate clause.

*Some of the children went home early **but** the others remained **because** they had no transport.*

first coordinate clause   coordinating conjunction   second coordinate clause   subordinating conjunction   subordinate clause

The Structure of Sentences tells you about the Target Audience

1) The length and complexity of sentences can be varied according to the **content** and **audience** of a text.

2) A good example of contrasting sentence structures is the difference between **broadsheet** and **tabloid** newspapers.

BROADSHEET NEWSPAPER

The scientific community is under the microscope as it nears hybrid embryo creation.
(Complex sentence: main clause + subordinate clause)

This is a serious ethical issue since it questions the very nature of what it is to be human.
(Complex sentence: main clause + subordinate clause)

The intention to find new ways of treating diseases that have so far proved untreatable is clearly laudable, but the magnitude of the moral issue can't be ignored, as the procedure will involve destroying live embryos after fourteen days.
(Compound-complex sentence: main clause + main clause + subordinate clause)

TABLOID NEWSPAPER

Mad scientists are on the verge of creating monsters.
(Simple sentence)

They will take the sperm and eggs of humans and animals and mix them up.
(Compound sentence: coordinate clause + coordinate clause)

Living embryos will be trashed after fourteen days.
(Simple sentence)

3) The writers create a different **mood** and **tone** depending on the types of sentences they use. They're intended to appeal to different **audiences**.

4) The first example is more complex — it has a **measured** and **serious tone**. The second, relatively simple set of sentences is more **emotive** and **subjective**.

Sentences

You can **Classify Sentences** by their **Function**

Sentences have **four** functions.

1) DECLARATIVES

- **Declarative** sentences are statements that **give information**, e.g. ⟶

> *This summer was the hottest on record.*
> *I don't like cheese.*

2) IMPERATIVES

- **Imperative** sentences **give orders**, **instructions**, **advice** and **directions**.
- They **start** with a **main verb** and **don't** have a **subject**, e.g. ⟶

> *Go left and it's first on your right.*
> *Answer one question from each section.*

3) INTERROGATIVES

Interrogative sentences ask **questions**.

- Some questions are formed by **inverting** (swapping round) the **verb** and the **subject** of a sentence.

E.g. *You are coming out tonight.* ⟶ *Are you coming out tonight?*

Subject **Verb** **Main verb** **Verb** **Subject** **Main verb**

- Interrogatives can start with *wh-* words, e.g. ⟶

> *Where are you going?*
> *When will you be back?*

- They can also be added to the **end of a statement**. These are called **tag questions**, e.g. ⟶

> *It's cold, **isn't it**?*
> *She said she was on her way, **didn't she**?*

- In **spoken discourse** you can turn **declarative statements** into questions using **stress** and **intonation**. This is called a **rising inflection**, e.g. ⟶

> *He will get better?*

4) EXCLAMATIVES

- **Exclamative** sentences have an **expressive function** — they convey the force of a statement, and end with an **exclamation mark**, e.g. ⟶

> *I will not do this any more!*
> *That was fantastic!*

Practice Questions

Q1   What does a simple sentence have to contain?

Q2   Give an example of a compound-complex sentence, and label the different types of clauses and conjunctions.

Q3   Describe the differences between sentence structures typically used in broadsheet and tabloid newspapers.

Q4   What are imperative sentences?

Q5   What is a tag question?

Q6   Give an example of an exclamative sentence.

What's the longest sentence in the English language? A levels...

Who would have thought that learning about sentences would turn out to be so interesting. Try comparing a few tabloid and broadsheet newspapers and you'll really be able to see the difference in the sentence structures they use. And while you're at it, look for some examples of minor, simple, compound, complex and compound-complex sentences too.

Morphology

Here's a nice treat for you — a couple of pages all about how prefixes and suffixes are used to create new words. In fact, I think these are my two favourite pages in the whole section, so I hope you like them too. Enjoy.

Morphemes are the Basic Units that make up words

1) **Morphology** is the study of **word formation**. It looks at how the **form** of a word **changes** because of **grammar**, and how the **meaning** of a word can **change** by adding an **affix** — a **unit** of a word like *un-* or *-ness*.

2) The separate units that make up words are called **morphemes**.

- Simple words are **morphemes** in their own right, such as *man*, *dog*, *ignore* and *journey*. They **can't** be **broken down** any further into meaningful units, e.g. *ig+nore*. They're called **free morphemes**, or **base**, **root** or **stem** forms.

- **Bound morphemes** are morphemes that are **not** words on their **own**. They're things like *-ful*, *-s*, *-ness* and *-est*, which can be added to **free** morphemes to create words like *thankful*, *cups*, *darkness* and *largest*.

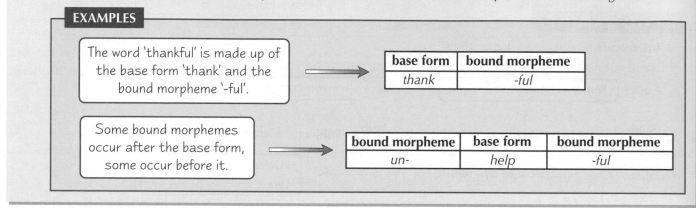

EXAMPLES

The word 'thankful' is made up of the base form 'thank' and the bound morpheme '-ful'.

base form	bound morpheme
thank	*-ful*

Some bound morphemes occur after the base form, some occur before it.

bound morpheme	base form	bound morpheme
un-	*help*	*-ful*

Prefixes can create New Words in the same Word Class

Prefixes are **morphemes** added to the start of a word. They change the **meaning** of nouns, verbs, adjectives and adverbs.

prefix	noun	new word
dis- →	parity →	*disparity*

prefix	verb	new word
inter- →	act →	*interact*

prefix	adjective	new word
ir- →	relevant →	*irrelevant*

prefix	adverb	new word
super- →	naturally →	*supernaturally*

Suffixes can change a word's Class and Meaning

Suffixes are **morphemes** added to the **end** of a word.

Suffixes and prefixes are both types of affix.

The tables below show how you form different words and word classes by adding **different suffixes** to the **base form**.

1) Base form is a **noun**:

noun	adjective	verb	adverb
type	*typical*	*typify*	*typically*

2) Base form is an **adjective**:

adjective	noun	verb	adverb
legal	*legality*	*legalise*	*legally*

3) Base form is a **verb**:

verb	noun	adjective	adverb
explode	*explosion*	*explosive*	*explosively*

Marjorie put a brave face on it, but she really didn't like the objects affixed to her head.

Morphology

Adding Morphemes to existing words is called Affixation

Affixes are **bound morphemes** that are added to words. There are **two** kinds of affixation — **inflectional** and **derivational**.

Inflectional affixation

1) **Inflectional affixation** changes the **grammar** of the word — e.g. its **number** or **tense**.

2) Inflectional affixes are always **suffixes** (they go after the base).
   For example, *pushed*. The bound morpheme *-ed* attaches to the verb *push* to change the action from the **present tense** to the **past tense**.

3) Here are some common kinds of inflectional affixation:

Plural *-s* (also *-ies*, *-oes*)	*dogs, ladies, tomatoes*	**Past participle** *-ed*	*He has recovered*
Possessive *-'s*	*Bernie's car*	**Present participle** *-ing*	*He is recovering*
Third person singular *-s*	*She says*	**Comparative** *-er*	*Quicker*
Past tense *-ed*	*He recovered*	**Superlative** *-est*	*Quickest*

Derivational affixation

1) Derivational affixation has a **semantic function** — it changes the **meaning** of a word.

2) The **noun** *player* is formed by adding the **suffix** *-er* to the **verb** *play*. The word changes from being an **action** to the **performer** of the action.

3) **Prefixes precede** (go before) the **base form**, **suffixes** come at the end — both can **change** the meaning of a word:

Prefix	Meaning	Example	Suffix	Meaning	Example
auto-	self	***auto**biography*	*-archy*	leadership	*hier**archy***
inter-	between	***inter**active*	*-less*	absence of	*shame**less***
un-	not, opposite	***un**necessary*	*-phobia*	fear	*claustro**phobia***

Morphology and Coining Words

Coining is the general term for creating words (see p. 20). Many new words are formed through **derivational affixation**. Here are a few different ways that new words can be coined:

1) **Clipping** — sometimes prefixes or suffixes are **dropped**. For example, *the gymnasium* is now usually referred to as *the gym*, and you're more likely to say *phone* than *telephone*.

2) **Compounds** — new words are created by **combining** two free morphemes, e.g. *mankind, blackbird* and *sleepwalk*.

3) **Back-formation** — this involves a free morpheme that **looks like** it has a suffix, like *editor*, being adapted to create a word like *edit*. **Historically** the word *editor* is a **free morpheme**, but the verb *edit* has been created **from** it. This is also true of *writer* (historically a free morpheme) inspiring the verb *write*.

4) **Blends** — new words are also created by **fusing** two words into one. These words are referred to as **blends**. For example, *alcoholic* has been fused with *chocolate* to form *chocoholic*, and with *shopping* to form *shopaholic*.

Practice Questions

Q1   What is a morpheme?

Q2   Give three examples of words that have been formed using prefixes.

Q3   Explain how suffixes can change the class of a word.

Q4   What's the difference between inflectional and derivational affixation?

Q5   Explain three ways that new words can be coined.

Aren't clipping and back-formation something hairdressers do?...

See, I told you these pages were going to be good. I don't know about you, but that mention of blending has put me in the mood for a nice refreshing milkshake. So once you're sure you've learned everything on these pages, why not have a break and go and make yourself one — if it's banoffee, you're blending words too, so it's even better.

Phonology and Phonetics

These cheeky little pages are all about different sounds in English, and the effects that they can create. Lots to take in here, but it's really useful background stuff, and nothing you won't have heard before in AS and in real life too.

Phonology and Phonetics are Different

Phonology

1) **Phonology** is the study of the **sound systems** of languages, in particular the **patterns** of sounds.

2) It focuses on **units** of sound, called **phonemes** (see below).

3) Unlike phonetics, in phonology you **don't** look at **differences** of **articulation**, e.g. if someone pronounces *stupid* as *shtupid*, the *s* and *sh* are still classed as the **same phoneme**, because the different pronunciation doesn't create a **different meaning**.

Phonetics

1) **Phonetics** is the study of how speech sounds are **made** and **received**.

2) It covers all **possible sounds** that the human vocal apparatus (vocal chords, tongue, lips, teeth, etc) can make.

3) It focuses on **differences** in **articulation**, e.g. different accents.

This is the International Phonetic Alphabet (IPA). It's used for writing all the possible phonemes (sounds) that humans can make in any language. Slanting brackets are used to distinguish between phonemes. See p. 64 for more on this.

Phonemes are Units of Sound

1) The **smallest units** of **sound** are called **phonemes**. There are only about **44** phonemes in English, and combinations of them make up **all** the **possible** words and sounds in the language.

2) For example, the word *cat* has **three** phonemes — /k/ (like the *c* in *coat*), /ae/ (like the *a* in *bat*) and /t/ (like the *t* in *toy*). By **changing** one of these phonemes (e.g. /f/ for /k/) you can create a new word, *fat*.

3) The 26 letters of the **alphabet** can express **all** the possible sounds in English, e.g. **pairs** of letters (**digraphs**) like *sh-* and *ch-* can be used to represent **single phonemes**.

4) The study of phonemes is divided into **vowel sounds** and **consonant sounds**.

Vowel Sounds

1) There are about **twenty vowel sounds** in English, even though there are only **five** vowels in the alphabet.

2) E.g. the vowel *a* has a different sound depending on the word in which it appears. In *ape* it sounds different to when it's in *sat, care* and *saw*.

3) Vowel sounds are usually in the **centre** of a **syllable**, e.g. b<u>a</u>g, c<u>oa</u>t.

4) When a vowel sound is spoken, the **vocal tract** is always **open** — the **airway** is clear and your **vocal chords** rub together to 'voice' the sound. Vowel sounds are made by **altering** the **shape** of the **mouth**. The way vowel sounds are **pronounced varies** in **different** regions. This is how people can tell the difference between accents.

Consonant Sounds

1) The number of **consonant sounds** in English is close to the **actual** number of **consonants** in the **alphabet**.

2) Consonants are mostly found at the **edges** of **syllables**, e.g. <u>b</u>oy<u>s</u>, <u>g</u>irl<u>s</u>. Sometimes they can appear in **sequences** of three or four consonants **together**, e.g. <u>str</u>ing or twel<u>fth</u>.

3) Unlike vowels, they're mostly articulated by **closing** the vocal organs.

4) Some consonants are formed by **vibration** of the vocal chords, e.g. /b/ and /n/. The amount of vibration depends on the **position** of the consonant within the word. At the end of the word, the consonant is less pronounced. Other consonants don't use the vocal cords at all, such as /p/ and /s/.

Words are made up of Syllables

Syllables are a word's **individual units** of pronunciation. They are normally **combinations** of consonants and vowels.

1) The **centre** of a syllable is usually a **vowel sound**, e.g. b<u>u</u>n, t<u>y</u>ke.

2) Syllables can have one or more **consonants before** the **vowel**, e.g. <u>b</u>e, <u>sl</u>ow.

3) Many syllables have one or more consonants **following** the **vowel**, e.g. a<u>nt</u>.

4) They can also have consonants before **and** following the vowel, e.g. <u>play</u>, <u>read</u>.

5) **Monosyllabic** words have **one syllable**, e.g. *plate, car*. **Polysyllabic words** have **more than one** syllable, e.g. *amazing* (a-maz-ing), *cryogenic* (cry-o-gen-ic).

Phonology and Phonetics

Words Sound Different when they're Connected

Words are often pronounced **differently** than you'd expect when you see them **written down**. This is because spoken language **combines** and **runs** sounds together.

Elision is when sounds are **left out**.
1) It happens especially in **rapid speech**, with words that have **clusters** of **consonants** or **syllables**.
2) For example, *library* is usually pronounced *libry*, and *everything* can become *evrythn*.

Assimilation is when sounds that are next to each other become **more alike**.
1) This happens especially in **rapid speech**, because it makes the words **easier** to say quickly.
2) For example, in the word *handbag*, *hand* becomes *ham*, to make it **easier** to **pronounce** with the syllable *bag*.

Liaison is when a **sound** is **inserted between** words or syllables to help them run **together** more smoothly.
1) For example — pronouncing /r/ at the **end of words**. When a word ending with **r** is **followed** by a word that **begins** with a **vowel**, the /r/ is **pronounced**, e.g. *mother ate* sounds like *mother rate*.
2) This is to avoid a gap between the words, known as a **hiatus**.
3) Sometimes it's easier to link words with /r/ even if there's no r in the spelling — e.g. *media(r) interest*.

Phonological Frameworks are used to Analyse Sound Patterns

Part of **phonology** involves looking at how sounds can convey **meaning** and **association**.

1) **Rhythm** is very clear in **poetry**. Lines are often **constructed** so that the **stress** falls on **important** words, emphasising their meaning, e.g. *But to **go** to **school** in a **summer** morn, / Oh! it **drives** all **joy** away.* **Advertising** also uses rhythm, particularly in **slogans**, to help the audience **remember** the **product**.

2) **Rhyme** is when words have **similar endings**. It's usually associated with poetry and songs, but it's also used in planned speeches and in advertising. The rhyming words in a speech or text always **stand out**, and their meanings are often **linked**.

3) **Alliteration** is where two or more words close to each other **begin** with the **same sound**, e.g. *six sizzling sausages*.

4) **Assonance** is when the **vowel sounds** in the middle of two or more words are similar, e.g. *spoke* and *hope*. When vowel sounds **clash** with each other it's known as **dissonance**, e.g. *ham-fisted*.

5) Alliteration and assonance are used in **creative writing** to **emphasise** words and show that the **meaning** is **linked** in some way. They're also used in **persuasive writing** to make phrases catchy and more memorable.

6) **Onomatopoeia** — this is when a word **sounds like** the noise it describes, e.g. *buzz, pop, bang, snap*.

7) Sometimes sounds can appear **symbolic** for other reasons, e.g. **closed vowels** in words like *chip* and *little* can suggest smallness, while **open vowels** in words like *vast* and *grand* can suggest largeness. It's not always the case, but it's worth noting **sound symbolism** like this when you're analysing a text.

Practice Questions

Q1 What is the difference between a phoneme and a syllable? Give examples of both.
Q2 Explain how words may sound different when they're said next to each other.
Q3 Define the following terms: onomatopoeia, assonance and alliteration.

Essay Question

Q1 Find a magazine article and discuss the effect of phonological features in the text.

Frank's late for his dinner — why doesn't he phoneme...

I mean, it's the third time this week. Anyone would think he doesn't like eel and mushroom baguettes — actually that's disgusting. Anyway, remind yourself what phonemes are, how syllables build words, how words are connected in speech, and of the importance of the phonological framework. Then, if you're lucky, I'll make you a sandwich... yum.

Phonemic Transcription

Line your stomachs for some particularly meaty pages now — the real spoken language stuff, complete with all the funny symbols and everything. So fasten your chinstraps, put down that weasel, and all hail the International Phonetic Alphabe

Phonemic Symbols express the Sounds of the language

Here is a list of the phonemic symbols that represent the **basic sounds** of the English language. You don't have to memorise them, but you should be **familiar** with the ones that are likely to be different across **regional accents** — mainly the **vowels**. This list gives you examples of the sounds of English as they would be pronounced in **RP**.

Consonants of English

/f/ = friend, tou**gh**	/ʃ/ = **sh**ape, bru**sh**	/b/ = **b**id, ro**b**	/n/ = me**n**, **sn**ake
/v/ = **v**enue, **v**illain, ha**ve**	/ʒ/ = lei**s**ure, vi**s**ion	/d/ = **b**ad, **d**eman**d**	/ŋ/ = ha**ng**er, lo**ng**
/θ/ = **th**ink, **th**rough	/h/ = **h**aunt, **h**it, be**h**ind	/g/ = ba**g**, **g**ain	/l/ = **l**arge, be**ll**
/ð/ = ei**th**er, **th**em, **th**ough	/p/ = **p**ot, ti**p**, s**p**at	/tʃ/ = **ch**urch, hun**ch**	/j/ = **y**ou, **y**acht
/s/ = **s**ell, dot**s**, cro**ss**es	/t/ = **t**op, pi**t**, s**t**ep	/dʒ/ = **j**udge, **g**in, **j**ack	/w/ = **wh**at, **o**nce, s**w**itch
/z/ = **z**oo, dog**s**, squee**z**e	/k/ = **k**ick, **c**ope, s**cr**ew	/m/ = **m**iddle, s**m**ell	/r/ = **r**oad, d**r**y

Short vowels of English

/ɪ/ = t**i**p, b**u**sy, h**i**ss
/e/ = sh**e**d, **a**ny
/æ/ = c**a**t, h**a**d, b**a**nk
/ɒ/ = w**a**nt, r**o**bot
/ʌ/ = c**u**p, s**o**n, bl**oo**d
/ʊ/ = w**oo**d, p**u**t, b**oo**k
/ə/ = **a**bout, bal**a**nce

Long vowels of English

/i:/ = sh**ee**p, h**ea**t
/ɑ:/ = c**ar**, b**al**m
/ɜ:/ = b**ir**d, h**ear**d
/ɔ:/ = p**or**t, t**al**k
/u:/ = f**oo**d, shr**ew**d

Diphthongs of English

/eɪ/ = gr**ea**t, d**ay**	/əʊ/ = b**oa**t, h**o**me
/aɪ/ = f**ly**, br**igh**t	/ɪə/ = h**ere**, n**ear**
/ɔɪ/ = b**oy**, n**oi**se	/eə/ = st**are**, **air**
/aʊ/ = c**ow**, h**ou**se, g**ow**n	/ʊə/ = m**ore**, p**oor**

Don't panic — you don't have to transcribe anything, OR learn all these symbols off by heart. You'll get a copy of the symbols in the exam paper, so you can use them in your answers if it's appropriate. You could also use them in your coursework.

There are different types of Vowel Sound in English

There are three **distinct types** of vowel sound in English — short vowels, long vowels and diphthongs (two vowels in one).

*bin /bɪn/, ban /bæn/ and bun /bʌn/ are examples of **short vowel sounds**.*
*bean /bi:n/, barn /bɑ:n/ and burn /bɜ:n/ are examples of **long vowel sounds**.*

Two vowel sounds can also be **fused together**, to form a **diphthong**.

*bite /baɪt/, bait /beɪt/ and boat /bəʊt/ are examples of **diphthongs**.*

Phonemic symbols provide a valuable way of demonstrating the **differences in sound** — something that you can't necessarily show by the way the **words** are **spelled** — think of *read* /ri:d/ and *read* /red/.

You can use phonemic symbols in Language Analysis

The standard practice when you're including a phonemic transcription is to start it on a **new line** so it can be read easily, leaving spaces **between the words** as in normal writing.

To give you an idea, this is how the definition of phonetics from p. 62 would look in transcription:

Phonetics is the study of how speech sounds are made and received
fənetɪks ɪz ðə stʌdɪ ɒv haʊ spi:tʃ saʊndz ɑ: meɪd ænd rɪsi:vd

And this is how part of the definition of phonology would look:

Phonology is the study of the sound systems of languages
fənɒlədʒɪ ɪz ðə stʌdi ɒv ðə saʊnd sɪstəmz ɒv læŋgwɪdʒɪz

Phonemic Transcription

Phonetics shows the Differences between Accents

Here's a sentence as an example:

> ### How are you feeling today?

A phonemic transcription of this sentence in **Received Pronunciation** (RP) would look like this:

> haʊ ɑ juː fiːlɪŋ tədeɪ

However, the same sentence spoken in a **Scottish accent** would appear like this:

> hɒʊ er ju fiːlɪn tɪde:

A **Geordie accent** would be different again:

> hu: ɔ juː fiːlɪn tɪdɪə

And so would a **West Country accent**:

> aʊ ɑːr juː fiːlɪŋ tədeɪ

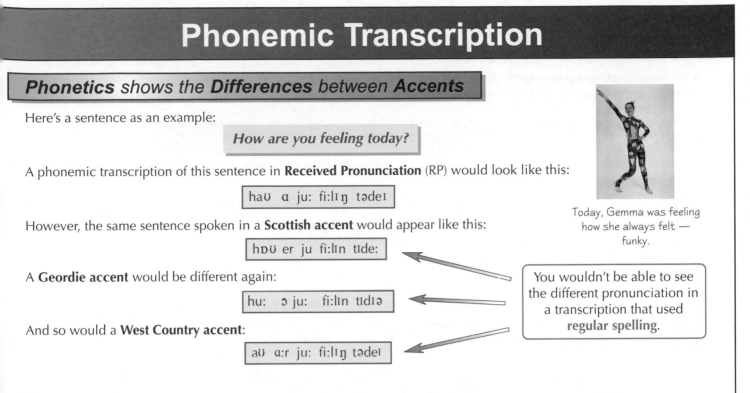

Today, Gemma was feeling how she always felt — funky.

You wouldn't be able to see the different pronunciation in a transcription that used **regular spelling**.

Phonemic Symbols can identify Specific Features of Pronunciation

If you're using a phonemic transcription in some analysis, you can record specific **linguistic features** very accurately. This is especially useful if you're looking at **accent** and **dialect**. Here are a couple of examples:

Glottal Stops — e.g. in the word *matter*

- The 't' sound in *matter* often **isn't articulated** with the tongue.
- Instead the speaker will use what is known as a **glottal stop**. This is technically a movement of the **vocal chords** that mainly (in English) acts as a **substitute** for the non-pronunciation of the 't'.
- The glottal stop is shown in phonemic transcriptions by a symbol that looks a bit like a **question mark** /ʔ/. So *matter* would look like this in transcription: /mæʔɒ/

Elision — e.g. in the phrase *Alright mate?*

- This greeting is likely to be said **quickly**, and this will result in **elision** (see p. 63).
- Some sounds will be **left out altogether**, even though they're included when the phrase is spelled out.
- A phonemic transcription of what is actually spoken might look like this: /ɒwɔɪmaɪʔ/

Practice Questions

Q1   What are the three distinct types of vowel sound in English?

Q2   What is a diphthong?

Q3   What is a glottal stop?

Essay Question

Q1   Explain, with examples, why a phonemic transcription is more useful in highlighting the differences between regional accents than a direct transcription of a conversation or interview.

It's a shame no one coined 'diphthong' as an insult first...

Can you imagine if you were able to call someone a 'massive diphthong'? That would be brilliant. It's a real shame that it's a very technical term for two vowel sounds realised as one. Anyway, I'm sure you'll get over it. Phonemic symbols are really useful for highlighting the differences between regional speakers — so it's pretty handy to be familiar with them, at least.

Register and Mode

A couple of quite straightforward pages to end this section with. It's really all stuff that you already know just from being aware of different types of language, and generally being alive. So go forth and state the obvious...

Register is the *Type* of *Language* used in different *Situations*

Registers are the different **varieties** of language used in different **situations**. Deciding which register is **appropriate** to use depends on several factors.

Audience
- This is to do with the **relationship** between the speaker or writer and the audience.
- For example, if the speaker or writer knows the audience personally, the **register** they use will usually be quite **informal**. It might include informal lexis, like slang and abbreviations.
- This may be more apparent in informal speech than in informal writing.

Purpose
- For example, a **report** will use a **formal register**, as its **purpose** is to convey information accurately.
- When the purpose is more **persuasive**, e.g. an advert, the register will often be more **informal** as the text needs to get the audience's attention in order to persuade them.

Field
- This is the subject being talked about.
- For example, if the topic is **football**, the **lexis** will include words linked to football, like *match, penalty,* etc.
- Some fields have a large specialist lexicon (stock of words), like **biochemistry**. Most workplaces have their own lexicon connected solely with that field, from car repair shops to hospitals.

Form
- For example, business letters will be written in a **formal register**.
- Text messages, on the other hand, tend to use a more **informal register**.

> Whether the register is **appropriate** depends on the **context** it's used in — using an **informal register** in a **formal situation** is **inappropriate** because it could seem **disrespectful** or **rude**. Using **formal language** in an **informal situation** could sound **unfriendly** and **stuffy**.

Registers Vary in terms of *Lexis*, *Grammar* and *Phonology*

Different **registers** use different **lexis** and **grammar**, and the way they're **pronounced** can **vary** too. For example:

Lexis
- A conversation between two **specialists** would contain **technical vocabulary** that they would both understand.
- For example, the lexis in the registers used by **mechanical** and **medical** specialists would be very different.

Grammar
- **Register** can affect syntax — the **structure** of clauses and **complexity** of sentences.
- Some registers even have grammatical constructions that are **specific** to them, like the legal register (known as **legalese**), which uses lots of clauses and mainly passive sentences.

Phonology
- This is to do with how the words in a particular **register** are **pronounced**.
- The **informal register** people use when speaking to friends often involves things like dropping the <h> from words like *have* and missing a <g> off words with the *ing* suffix, like *thinking*.
- Generally speaking, the more **formal** a situation is the more likely people are to **modify** their **accent** so it's closer to **Received Pronunciation** (see p. 27).

Register and Mode

Modes can be Written or Spoken

Written modes

1) Written modes include letters, essays, novels, recipes and reports. Written modes tend to be the **most formal**.

2) In written modes the words have to make the **meaning** clear, because there's no opportunity for **non-verbal communication** between the writer and the reader.

3) Sometimes writers try to convey **prosodic features** like tone, intonation and pitch to make the meaning clearer, using **features** like *italicising*, <u>underlining</u>, CAPITALISATION, and **punctuation** like exclamation marks.

Spoken modes

1) Spoken modes are things like interviews, broadcasts and presentations. Spontaneous speech (like a conversation between friends) is normally the **least formal** mode.

2) In **spoken modes** speakers can rely on **non-verbal communication** like gestures and **prosodic features** to get their point across.

3) The grammar of informal speech is often **disjointed** — it contains lots of **interruption** and **incomplete sentences**. It also contains **non-fluency features** (things that interrupt the flow of speech) like **self-correction**, **pauses**, **repetition**, **fillers** (*you know, sort of, I mean*) and **false starts**.

4) Speech also tends to contain **phatic expressions** (small talk expressions that have a **social function**, so their meaning isn't particularly important, like *hello* and *how's things?*).

Multi-Modal Texts contain Features of both Speech and Writing

Lots of texts are a **mixture** of **spoken** and **written** modes, especially electronic texts like **emails** and **text messages**.

1) These are **written modes** that can contain elements of **spoken language**, e.g. **phatic communication** like *hello* and *bye*.

2) Very **informal** emails or messages between friends contain **phonetic spellings**, like *b4* for *before*, and *u* for *you*.

3) **Formal** business emails still tend to be **less formal** than **letters** — they tend not to use **conventions** like writing the sender's address at the top. **Paragraphs** and **sentences** tend to be **shorter**.

Modes can be Classified in Different ways

Different modes can be **grouped** according to the following **approaches**:

1) **Continuum classification** — position on a **scale** that places written Standard English at one end and spoken informal speech at the other. In the middle are multi-modal texts like email.

2) **Typology** — grouping together genres that have **characteristics** or **traits** in common, e.g. sports commentaries, music reviews, formal interviews, novels, poems, etc.

3) **The dimensions approach** — looking at different aspects of modes, e.g. lexis, grammar and structure to analyse the level of formality in a certain text.

Practice Questions

Q1 What impact can audience have on register?

Q2 Outline how registers can vary in terms of lexis and grammar.

Q3 Outline four typical features of spoken modes.

Q4 Classify these three types of language by placing them on a continuum from least formal to most formal: text message to family member, business letter, transcript of a conversation between a teacher and a pupil.

Stod moding and ged od wid id...

When I was at primary school, we all thought it was a real treat if we were allowed to go and collect the class register from the office. Weird. Anyway, once you're sure you know everything on these pages, that's the end of the section. So you can give yourself a pat on the back, take a deep breath, and then you're ready to move on to the next section.

Choosing a Topic

*For one of your pieces of coursework you'll have to produce a **language investigation**.*
This involves exploring and analysing language data using a variety of methods. Bet you can't wait...

You need to find a Suitable Topic

You need to have some idea about what **aspect** of **language** you want to study.

1) Think about your choice of topic so that you don't end up wasting time or getting stuck. This is probably the **most important** point of all — think ahead and be **realistic**. You'll need to produce **enough work** to satisfy the unit's requirements, but you don't want to choose too **wide-ranging** a task or one that ends up being **too demanding** and **impossible to complete**. Your teacher can help you with this.

This section gives you some general advice about how to carry out an investigation. You should still check the details with your teacher, in case they change.

2) It's best to pick something that really **interests you**. If you know the subject well, you should be able to work out whether it will offer enough **scope**, and if you'll be able to get **enough suitable information**.

3) Make sure you choose a topic where the data you need will be **accessible**. If you can't find **enough information** about your topic, then you're bound to struggle.

4) Your investigation should be **1750-2500** words long, excluding data and appendices.

Different Types of Investigation look at different Aspects of language

1) Being able to identify **different types** of language investigation and applying them to the area you're thinking of studying will help you to **narrow down** your topic.

2) It can also **highlight potential problems** (e.g. if your method is going to give you enough suitable information about your topic) before you get started.

3) This list of different investigation types should help you focus on a more specific area for your study.

Language Based

An investigation that looks at a **particular type of language** in order to determine something about its distinctive features.

> **For example:**
> *Looking at regional variations in English by recording people from different parts of the country reading or speaking, and analysing these examples.*

Function Based

An investigation that focuses on the **use of language**, and how one type of language achieves a particular effect.

> **For example:**
> *The specific language techniques used in political speeches to persuade, convince or influence an audience so that they end up sharing the point of view of the speaker.*

Attitudes Based

An investigation that focuses on **reactions** and **responses** to a particular type of language.

> **For example:**
> *You could look at how people across different age groups feel about the language of teenagers, or their attitudes to slang words etc. You'd have to identify specific groups to talk to in relation to this though.*

User Based

An investigation focusing on the **people** who use a particular type of language — how they use it and how it affects them and those around them.

> **For example:**
> *The jargon or sociolect used by people in a particular trade or profession, or in relation to a hobby or an area of personal interest.*

Choosing a Topic

You might find it *Easier* to stick to something you've *Already Studied*

Here are a few things that you'll have covered at **AS** or **A2** that you could investigate (but you don't have to — you can pick other topics). Make sure you **discuss** your **topic** with your **teacher** before you start.

LANGUAGE ACQUISITION	LANGUAGE IN SOCIAL CONTEXTS	LANGUAGE CHANGE
For example:	**For example:**	**For example:**
What role does the caregiver play in language development?	How are regional dialects perceived in schools?	How has a particular grammatical feature of English changed over time?
Is there an order in which children acquire features of language?	Do men and women use language differently?	How do people express their attitudes towards language change?

Think about **How** you're going to **Investigate Your Topic**

There are 3 main ways you can set up your investigation. You can suggest a **theory** (hypothesis) that you want to prove or discredit, set yourself a **specific question** to answer, or go for a **study** based on discussing a certain area and its features.

1) **Hypothesis** based topics

- A hypothesis is a statement that proposes a **possible explanation** for some issue but doesn't offer proof, e.g: *If language changes through generations, then there will be identifiable language differences across three generations of the same family.*
- A hypothesis based investigation tests the hypothesis by collecting data, and then by **evaluating** the results.

2) **Question** based topics

- Questions can be based on something you've **observed** about the way language functions, or how it's used, that can then be **explored** in more detail.
- Any question that you set yourself should be clear and make it **obvious** what you plan to look at, e.g: *To what extent is the language of children's television adapted to assist or influence their linguistic development?*

3) **Descriptive** topics

- A descriptive language investigation focuses on **comparing** and **evaluating** data without trying to prove a point or investigate a theory. Instead of analysing results, you **comment** on the **linguistic features** in your data, e.g. you might look at how verbs have changed over time, and discuss why this might have happened.

Think about how you'll **Get Your Information**

1) The **methodology** is the approach you use to **obtain your information**. It needs to be carefully planned in advance, because in your write-up you need to **describe** and **analyse** the process in detail and comment on what worked well — as well as what didn't.

2) These are the methodologies you might use for the types of topic listed above:

- For a **hypothesis based topic** you might **record** and **transcribe** samples of speech in order to prove a theory about certain speakers.
- For a **question based topic** you might look at **different types** of language and suggest which is most **effective** for its purpose.
- For a **descriptive topic** you might look back at the archives of selected newspapers to **compare** and **evaluate** the style of writing and presentation methods between old examples and up-to-date ones.

A seriously flawed methodology for studying the language of birds was about to teach Terry a very unpleasant lesson.

Time to pic a topic...

This stuff can all seem a bit daunting — you want to choose something vaguely interesting that isn't going to require shed loads of extra work, but isn't too easy either. Tricky. But it's not impossible. Just find a topic that isn't going to completely bore your brains out, and once you get stuck into it you'll soon become an enthusiastic linguist. That's the idea, anyway...

Collecting Data

There are plenty of ways to collect data — but you need to make sure that your collection method gives you the best chance of getting what you need. If that happens to include the use of a sharp stick or forcing people to watch Noel Edmonds on TV for 6 hours, then so be it. Just kidding. Don't do that.

You should collect Primary and Secondary Language Data

Data is the **raw material** that you'll be collecting so that you've got something to write about in your investigation. There are **two types** you should look at:

1) **Primary Language Data** — data that can be obtained directly. For example — recordings of spoken language, samples of written language, lists of words used in conversation or in writing, examples of slang or dialect, and features of pronunciation.

2) **Secondary Language Data** — data from other sources that can tell you about language. For example — other people's research findings or newspaper articles about attitudes towards language. You should use it to support your argument, either by agreeing with it, or explaining why you think it's wrong.

There are Different Types of Primary Data

You'll collect **different types** of data depending on what you're studying. Use these terms in your coursework to describe the kind of data you've got and impress whoever marks it.

1 Comparative and Contrastive Data

This is when you study **two or more types** of data and **analyse** the **similarities** and **differences** between them. For example, you might compare and contrast the language of text messages with the language of emails.

2 Longitudinal Data

This is when data from **one source** is gathered over a period of **time** so that comparisons or contrasts can be made. For example, you might compare the language of news coverage from the past with news coverage from today.

You can use Different Methods to collect your data

1) Collecting Spoken Language Data

There are various different ways in which spoken language data can be collected.

• **Note-taking** — making notes as people are speaking.

• **Preparing a questionnaire on language use**. You can give a questionnaire to someone to fill in, or conduct an interview with them and fill in the answers yourself. You need to plan the questionnaire so that the person's answers demonstrate or discuss whatever feature of spoken language you've chosen to investigate.

• **Tape-recordings** — these could be of conversations between two people, or of a single person reading, speaking about a particular experience, or explaining their opinions on an issue. However, if you record someone without their knowledge, then you're **legally obliged** to obtain their **permission** afterwards, otherwise you can't use their responses as part of your investigation.

Collecting spoken language data is a **time-consuming** business. You might also have to transcribe recordings (in case you need a hard copy, or want to do a phonemic analysis). Doing this can be **useful** and will look really impressive, but you shouldn't spend loads of time doing it at the **expense** of the **other parts** of your investigation.

2) Collecting Written Language Data

Written language data is just any **written text**, e.g. fiction, media texts, emails. In theory, collecting written language data should be easier than collecting spoken language data, as long as it's fairly **concise** and **relevant** to your topic.

3) Combining Spoken and Written Language Data

You could also choose to analyse some of the **differences** between spoken and written language, either in everyday use or in language acquisition. For example, if you're looking at how children begin to develop their language skills, you could **record** their conversations and get **samples** of their writing/drawings.

Collecting Data

Questionnaires need to be Carefully Designed

1) First of all, you need to have a **clear idea** of what you want to gain from your questions. It may be better to avoid questions that only have a 'yes' or 'no' response (known as **closed questions**) if you're looking for evidence of linguistic **features** or **opinions** on language.

2) You could ask **open questions** that will encourage people to talk for a while, e.g. asking them for their **opinion**, encouraging them to talk about themselves or getting them to tell **anecdotes** or **stories**.

3) You need to decide **who to ask** in order to get the information you want — this will be your **sample**. You need to make sure that participants fit into the group that your research question has specified (e.g. differences between **male** and **female teenagers**), and design your questions so **everyone can answer them effectively**.

You have to do some Planning before conducting an Interview

There are a number of decisions to make **before** you start:

1) **Who** are you going to interview — just **one person**, or a number of people so that you end up with a wider **range** of responses (but potentially more work)?

2) Are you going to **record** the interview, in which case you'll need to **transcribe** it later, or are you going along with just a notebook for **note-taking**?

3) Are you going to conduct your interview **face-to-face**, over the **phone**, or in some other way, for example via the **Internet**?

> You'll also need to decide whether to ask for facts or opinions, or a combination of the two.

There are Problems with studying People

Whatever type of investigation and methodology you choose, collecting data from **other people** can be a bit tricky.

1) If they've been told exactly what the study is about, some participants can end up doing what **they think** the researcher wants them to, rather than **acting normally**.

2) Experimental situations aren't the most **normal experiences** at the best of times (it's pretty hard to just ignore a **camera** or a **microphone**, for example).

3) This is called the **observer's paradox** — the researcher can affect participants' reactions just by being present or making people aware they're being watched.

4) On the other hand, **not telling** participants what they should expect to experience can be **extremely unethical** — they have a right to be briefed on what the investigation is all about in case they're uncomfortable with the study.

The reaction to the 'language and the law investigation' was largely unfavourable.

Some Methods are better suited to certain Investigations

Language Based Investigation	You could collect **spoken** or **written** language data, or both. **Transcriptions**, particularly phonemic transcriptions, give you lots of **detail** but can be very **time-consuming**.
Function Based Investigation	For this type of investigation you'll need to use a **variety of sources**, so you can make **comparisons** between them.
Attitudes Based Investigation	This is the most likely type of investigation for using **secondary language data** (p. 70), as it's all about how people respond to the use of language in a particular **context**.
User Based Investigation	This type of investigation could use **various methods** of data collection. It could focus on spoken or written language in a **particular context**, or on a **combination** of the two.

You'll get the most natural responses if you ask about data-day stuff...

... like holidays, or biscuits, or walking the dog. You need to make sure your participants (if you've got any) are at ease, so they'll act naturally and not just say what they think you want them to. That's what the observer's paradox is all about — influencing your own results just by being in the same room. When are they going to invent that invisibility cloak...

Recording Data

When you've collected all the data you need, it's time to decide how you're going to present it in the context of your investigation. Serving suggestions include a nice salad garnish, or maybe a slice of lemon...

Be *Selective* with *Written Data*

1) If you're using **long pieces** of written data (like newspaper or magazine articles), then pick out some **shorter extracts** that **support** the point you're making. This saves you from having to do a detailed linguistic analysis of a huge amount of text, and should mean that the points you make are more **focused** on the topic.

2) Use **footnotes** (see p. 78) to draw attention to **specific linguistic features** in the text that **back up** the point you're making.

Spoken Data has to be *Transcribed*

1) Transcribing conversations is **tricky** — you'll probably need to listen to your recordings closely quite a **few times** before you write up your **final version**.

2) It's also quite **time-consuming**, so if you've recorded an **interview** or **conversation** as part of your data collection, you don't need to **transcribe** the whole thing. However, you do need to make sure that the extracts you choose are **relevant** to your investigation and that you **reproduce** what was said **accurately**.

3) Your data might include things like **pauses**, **repetitions** and **emphasis**. You should represent these features and include an **appendix** or **key** so the reader knows what it all means.

For example:

If you decide to look at differences in language because of **gender**, you could **record** a **conversation** between a **mixed group** of students at school or college.

This short **sample conversation** shows the things you could focus on when transcribing spoken language:

This extract is of an unsupervised conversation between 2 male students (1M and 2M) and 2 female students (1F and 2F), all aged 18. They have been asked to talk about 'holidays'.

1F: can't wait for mine (.) I haven't been away in <u>ages</u>

2F: I know (1) it'll be (.) just be <u>so</u> nice to be away

1M: // where you two going then

2F: er (.) France (1) like somewhere in the south I think

1M: // cool   // okay

1F: // the Dordogne

2F: it's well nice

2M: the <u>where</u> (1) what I've never heard of it

1M: that's because (.) because you're an idiot

2M: just because you're going camping in your garden

Don't use punctuation in your transcript — it isn't articulated, so it shouldn't be included. Use pauses or emphasis instead.

Key

(.) or (1) = *micropause or pause (number of seconds)*

// = *overlapping speech / interruptions*

<u>xxx</u> = *underlining — emphasis by speaker*

The transcript above includes the following features to make it as **clear** and **accurate** as possible:

- Identifies each speaker **individually** (1M, 2M, 1F and 2F) and gives the **context** of the conversation.
- Uses a **consistent symbol** to denote overlapping speech and interruptions (//).
- Underlines words that were **emphasised** by the speakers in the conversation.
- Uses **micropauses** and **numbers** to show **pauses** in the conversation e.g. (.) and (1).
- Lists all the features in a **key**.

If you're investigating **slang** or **dialect**, then you might want to include a **phonemic transcription** (see p. 64-65). If you're looking at **intonation** or **stress** you could use **extra symbols** to highlight the differences. If you do decide to do this, remember that although it can be really impressive, producing a very detailed transcription can take **absolutely ages**.

Analysing Data

You need to **Base Your Analysis** on a **Linguistic Framework**

You don't have to present **all the data** you've collected in your analysis — select specific parts of the data to **focus on** instead. Make sure you choose the parts that are **most relevant** to the subject of your investigation, and the bits that will make your discussion as clear and focused on the topic as possible.

1) Before you start analysing the data, try to group it into **categories**. You might decide to place some items of data from different sources together to illustrate some **similarities** and **differences**. This will help you when you're making **comparisons**, and it might work better than going through each piece of data systematically from beginning to end.

2) Next you'll need to decide what kind of **framework** you're going to use for your analysis:

   - **Lexis** — words and phrases.
   - **Semantics** — the meaning of words.
   - **Grammar** — structural relationships.
   - **Phonology** — sounds and how they're produced.
   - **Pragmatics** — social conventions of language and its implied meanings.
   - **Graphology** — the physical appearance of language.
   - **Discourse** — how texts are structured and made cohesive.

See p. 46 for more on language frameworks.

Despair set in as they realised Dan had selected the wrong framework.

3) The framework you choose should be the one that you feel will **best demonstrate** the points you're trying to make. You should try to keep to whichever one you choose, although topics do inevitably **overlap**.

Make sure you choose the **Right Framework**

It's important to choose a **relevant** framework to work with when you're analysing data. For example, it'd be pretty stupid to look at the graphology of a conversation. Here are a few suggestions:

> **Comparing written data** — if you're comparing language use over a period of time you may be focusing on **lexis** or **grammar**. A function or user-based topic might focus on **pragmatics**, **discourse** or **graphology** too.

> **Comparing spoken data** — a **phonological** framework would be an obvious choice for a topic focusing on slang or dialect, but you could use **lexical** or **grammatical** frameworks too.

> **Comparing spoken data to written data** — for language in everyday use, the question of **formality** versus **informality** is likely to come up, so you'll probably choose a **lexical** or **grammatical** framework. A topic on language development in the early years of childhood might also focus on lexis and grammar — you'd be looking for comparisons between **rates of development** of spoken and written language in those years.

Draw Conclusions from your **Analysis**

1) Ideally, you want to conclude your investigation by showing that you've found out **something new** and **worthwhile** that can be proved by the **evidence** you've presented.

2) You should **broaden** out your analysis to look at **other factors** that could have **influenced** the data. For example, you should consider the impact of **contextual factors**, like where a conversation took place, or the historical context a text was produced in.

3) There may be things you have to **leave open** because you can't fully prove them — e.g. with a hypothesis based topic you might find evidence that suggests a particular trend without providing **comprehensive proof**.

4) Your conclusions should always be **related** to your **evidence**, but they don't have to agree with your **original predictions**, or with any secondary sources you've looked at. The most important thing is that you **justify** what you say by showing how it's **supported** by your data.

Transcription might take ages, but it's worth sticking with it...

Do you think Rebecca Adlington invented swimming overnight? No — it took her years. The same goes for Lewis Hamilton and cars. Don't even get me started on how many rubbish breakfasts I had before I finally came up with the concept of putting milk on cereal. The point here, of course, is that it's worth it in the end. A thorough analysis will be too.

Writing Up the Investigation

*Now for the important part — producing a write-up of your investigation. Otherwise, it doesn't really exist...
There's a pretty standard layout for all of this, so it's not too tricky. Just be methodical and work through the sections.*

Start by **Explaining** your **Work (Introduction)**

1) First of all, you need to **explain your reasons** for choosing a particular area of study, including any advice or guidance from **other sources** that helped you towards this decision.

> Zimmerman and West's (1975) dominance model suggests that male speakers are responsible for 96% of interruptions in male-female conversations. As this research is now over 30 years old, I wish to investigate whether the model they proposed still applies to today's mixed-gender conversations.

2) Then you'll need to explain what **type** of **investigation** you've chosen, and whether it's hypothesis based, question based or descriptive — give **reasons** for these decisions too. You could also include some information about the data you've collected.

> This investigation will therefore deal with the following hypothesis: female students in mixed-gender conversations will compete with male speakers to dominate a conversation by non-supportive interruptions, not following rules of turn-taking, prolonging their own turns with non-verbal fillers, and instigating changes in conversation topic.

3) Finally you'll need to outline the **aims of your investigation** — what you set out to **discover** and **achieve**.

Explain **How** You **Collected** your **Data (Methodology)**

1) In this section you'll need to explain how you **obtained your data**, and what **decisions** you made as part of the process. For example, whether your data is **written**, **spoken** or a **combination of the two**, and why this is.

> The data for this investigation comes from a series of unsupervised conversations between male and female students. In order to investigate the effect of gender on these conversations, the participants were informed that they would be recorded, and given the neutral topic "holidays" to discuss.

2) You should then explain how you **designed your investigation**, together with the **techniques** you used in your research and the **language frameworks** you chose. You should explain why these techniques were **appropriate**, and outline any **problems** you encountered while you were collecting your data.

> As this investigation deals with how male and female participants respond to each other, the principle framework that will inform the discussion is that of pragmatics — how the conventions of spoken language are respected, followed or broken according to the gender of different speakers.

Present your **Findings** clearly **(Analysis)**

1) This should be one of the **largest sections** of your investigation. You need to give a **detailed** and **systematic analysis** and **interpretation** of the data you've collected.

2) To make this section easier to follow (and write), divide it into **subsections**, with **relevant subheadings** to show how it all fits together.

3) Most of your results will be presented as a **discussion**, but you can also include **charts or diagrams** to support your points — they make the analysis **clearer** and more **systematic**.

> In this conversation between male and female students, there were 25 instances in which the speakers interrupted each other or overlapped. As the table and graph show, these instances were fairly evenly spread — the male speakers account for 14 of the interruptions (56%), and the females for 11 (44%).

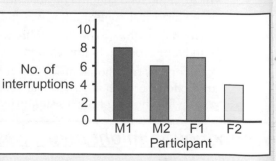

Participant	M1	M2	F1	F2
Interruptions	8	6	7	4
As % of total	32	24	28	16

Writing Up the Investigation

Bring your Results and Analysis Together (Conclusion)

1) In your conclusion you should explain what you've been able to **work out** from your **analysis**. You should refer back to the **aims** in your introduction section and say if they've been met, and what you've found out.

> This investigation tested the hypothesis that female speakers are as dominant as males in mixed-gender conversations. The evidence suggests that due to a similar frequency of non-supportive interruptions, topic shifting and disregarding turn-taking, female speakers are more similar to males than Zimmerman and West's dominance model suggests.

2) Whichever form of investigation you choose, you'll need to say if your **expectations** were met or not. If your findings aren't what you expect, **don't be afraid to admit it** — you can **discuss** why this might be the case, and you'll still get plenty of **credit**.

3) The point of this investigation is to reveal something **new** or of **interest**. However, in **relative terms**, your sample size and resources won't be **very big**, so be careful about boldly claiming that you've worked out everything there is to know about female conversational habits (for example).

> The evidence I have produced suggests that female speakers are just as likely as males to dominate conversations. This may reflect how gender roles in conversation are changing, and may mean that Zimmerman and West's (1975) dominance theory can be updated. However this is a very small sample so it is clear more research is needed.

4) If you can see a **potential** for **further study**, the end of your conclusion is a good place to suggest it.

Explain whether you could Improve your Investigation (Evaluation)

1) When you're evaluating your own work, **be honest** about the success of your investigation. Try and deal with some (if not all) of the following questions:

- Was the process of **data collection** easier or harder than you anticipated?
- How **effective** was your chosen method of **analysis**?
- Did you find you had **sufficient data** for your results to be **significant**?
- Did the information you came up with offer opportunities for **further research**?

> I tried to avoid the observer's paradox in this investigation by giving the participants a conversation topic and some written instructions rather than being present in the room. However the presence of the recording equipment may have affected the participants' conduct and made them feel more self-conscious than they would normally.

2) It's never particularly easy to criticise your own work, but you should try to **evaluate** the whole process — it looks really good if you can say what worked well and what you would improve if you did the investigation again.

Reference your Sources in the Bibliography

There's loads more on bibliographies on p. 79.

1) The **bibliography** is where you **acknowledge** every **secondary source** you've used. It's basically a big list of books and articles etc. that goes at the **end** of your investigation.

2) The easiest way to do it is to **keep a note** of every secondary source you use in relation to your investigation **as you go along**. Then you won't have to scrabble back through it all when you've finished.

You have to provide Copies of your Original Data (Appendices)

1) At the very end of your investigation, include any **extra information** that supports it, or that might be helpful to someone reading it. This could include **copies of questionnaires**, **transcripts of spoken data**, and **copies of written data**.

2) You should only include **primary research material** here — data that you've **collected yourself** during the course of your investigation.

"Ah, I see the problem here — you don't seem to have included your appendix."

Writing up is all very well, but make sure you write everything down too...

In fact, why is it called writing up? Just goes to show you can't trust the English language to make any sense whatsoever. On that revolutionary note, it's now your job to take a deep breath and start writing about your investigation (another 'write' preposition there). Remember — be thorough, methodical and accurate and the 'marks for' column will stack up just fine.

Writing a Media Text

For your other piece of coursework, you have to write an informative media text that's based on the broad subject focus of your language investigation. It should be 750-1000 words, and it should be aimed at a non-specialist audience.

You have to write an *Informative Media Text*

1) Your media text should be on the **same topic** as your **language investigation**. However, because it's for a different audience, you need to **re-present** the topic so that it's accessible to **non-specialists**.

2) What you write **doesn't** have to **reflect** what you found in your **language investigation**. This means it doesn't matter which order you do the tasks in.

3) Here are some examples of the type of text you could write.

- Newspaper editorial
- Magazine article
- Article for an online publication
- Blog
- Script for a radio or TV programme or podcast

Make sure you discuss your idea with your teacher before you start.

Make sure you *Research* your chosen *Genre*

1) You should do some **background reading** in the genre you choose, to give you tips on the appropriate **style** and **tone** to use.

2) Think about the **purpose** of your text too. It has to be **informative**, but it could have other purposes too, e.g. a magazine article could be written to **entertain** and **persuade** as well as **inform**.

3) Here are some general hints on the **structures** and **conventions** of a few different media texts:

1 *Tabloid Newspapers use Different language from Broadsheets*

If you're writing a newspaper article, you should think about whether it's for a **tabloid** or a **broadsheet** newspaper, as this will affect your **language choices**.

1) **Tabloid newspapers** are ones like *The Sun* and *The News of the World*. They tend to be written in an **informal register** and make their viewpoint very clear. They use quite **straightforward language**, which often contains features of **spoken English** like **slang** and **contractions**.

2) Tabloids have **less space** than **broadsheets**, so writers need to get the story across in as **few words** as **possible**. They also rely more on **grabbing** the reader's **attention** and **entertaining** them.

3) **Broadsheets** are newspapers such as *The Guardian* and *The Daily Telegraph*. They're aimed at **professional**, mostly **middle class readers**, so the **register** is more **formal** and articles tend to be **longer** (see p. 28 and p. 58).

2 *Some Online Texts are Less Formal than Printed ones*

Online texts can have different **purposes** and be written for different **audiences**. For example, an article that appeared on a newspaper's website, or one for people interested in linguistics, would probably be more **formal** than a **blog**.

1) A **weblog** (or **blog** for short) is a website which allows internet users to **publish** their writing online. These sites are usually **unregulated**, so the content is decided by the writer.

2) Many blogs take the form of **diaries** or **editorials**. They can be written **anonymously**, allowing writers to express views that they might otherwise keep to themselves. The language used can be forthright and confrontational.

3) More professional blogs use Standard English to mimic newspaper editorials and make them **accessible** to a wide audience. However, many bloggers use the **slang** and **shorthand** they'd use in a text message or email. It's probably best to stick mostly to **Standard English** if you write a blog for your media text.

3 *Scripted Language is Written to be Spoken*

You should bear these points in mind if you write a **radio** or **TV script**.

1) Because these texts are designed to be **spoken**, you could include some hints to the speaker on how it should be **performed**. For example, it could contain **prosodic features** like **pauses** and **emphasis** (you could use underlining, italics or capital letters for this).

2) If it's TV then you could include some **visual directions**, e.g. suggestions for how the performer should move.

Writing a Media Text

You need to Research Other People's Ideas

1) As well as looking at texts in your chosen genre, you should read other texts to see **what else has been said** about the topic you're covering.

2) These should be the same kinds of **secondary language data** (see p. 70) that you use in the **language investigation**. This could include things written for specialists, like books written by **linguists**. It could also include texts for **non-specialists**, e.g. newspaper articles written for much **wider audiences**. You could use the bibliography from a textbook or journal article to find some good sources.

> **Secondary sources**
>
> - Textbooks
> - Academic journals
> - Newspaper and magazine articles
> - Television or radio broadcasts
> - Web pages

3) It's a good idea to read some sources that show people's **attitudes** towards the aspect of language you're studying. Doing this can help you decide which **angle** to approach your coursework from, as well as providing you with material to **support** the points you make.

4) Remember that secondary sources can be useful even if you **disagree** with what they're saying. You can bring them up in your text and then explain why you think these views are wrong.

5) Using secondary sources can get you loads of marks. You need to show that you can **evaluate** and **synthesise** (bring together) ideas from different texts. Don't feel like it's cheating to include other people's ideas (as long as they've been properly acknowledged) — it shows you have the **skills** to **understand** the **main points** from a text and **use** them in a way that **fits** your **argument**.

Don't Plagiarise

1) It's good to use secondary sources in your text, but what you mustn't do is take words or ideas from other sources and pass them off as your own. This is **plagiarism**, and you can **fail** if you're caught doing it.

2) To avoid this you have to **acknowledge** any work that isn't your own, and credit where you got your ideas from.

3) You should reference everything you've read in your **footnotes** and **bibliography** (see p. 78-79). This can be quite time-consuming, but it's **absolutely essential**. The best way to do it is to make a **detailed note** of everything you read as you do it, then you can put it all together in your bibliography once you've finished. This will save you going back through all your secondary sources at the end.

Aim your text at a Non-Specialist Audience

One of the ways you can show that you've really understood the secondary sources you've read is by **re-wording** the information to suit a **different audience**. The exam board calls this **re-presentation**.

1) When you **re-present** information, it shows that you've understood all the texts you've studied. It's a way of proving that you can draw out the **most important ideas**, decide what's **relevant** to your **new audience**, and **deliver** it in a way that they'll **understand**.

2) Because you've studied the topic you're re-presenting, you're a **specialist**. But you have to write for a **non-specialist audience**, which means you should think about which technical terms you can use, and how much you'll need to explain to make sure they understand. Remember that your text should show off your **writing** and **editorial skills**, as well as your **subject knowledge**.

3) Usually you'll be re-presenting material to a **different audience** from the one your secondary sources were written for. For example, if you've been studying child language acquisition, you might read some **studies** on how children learn to read. But if you're then **re-presenting** this information for an article in a parenting magazine, you **wouldn't** include all the **specialist detail** and **terminology** you'd read. Instead, you'd give a much more **simple, user-friendly overview**.

MORE coursework???...

It seems a bit cheeky to make you do this as well as a language investigation, but that's exam boards for you. Mischievous little rascals they are. Why, only the other day one sneaked up behind me and poured a bucket of water over my head. I wouldn't have minded but I was actually in an exam at the time and it was a bit off-putting. Made the ink run and everything.

References and Bibliographies

It's important that you acknowledge your sources in both pieces of coursework. It's dull, but at least it's straightforward — there's a very specific way of doing it. Luckily for you, it's on these two pages. I wouldn't leave you hanging.

Include **All** your **References**

1) You have to include **references** in your investigation. It means that anyone reading or assessing your work can use the **same sources** as you have, and can check where you got your information from.

2) Referencing also provides **evidence** of the sources that you've consulted to widen your own **knowledge** and formulate your **hypothesis / research question**.

3) You have to include a list to show that you're not **plagiarising** — copying other people's work and/or ideas without **due acknowledgement** (see p. 77).

4) References let you **illustrate specific points**, and provide **support** for the arguments you're putting forward (or discrediting).

Make sure you **Understand** the **Terminology**

1) **Citations** and **footnotes** are the two main forms of *references*. They refer the reader to a **source** or **piece of information** that isn't in the **main body** of your text. If it's a citation, the information is highlighted **briefly** in the **same sentence**. If it's a footnote, the information is at the **foot of the page**.

2) A **bibliography** is the section at the end of the work where all the references are **drawn together** and listed in full. All sources **need to be acknowledged**, even if you don't specifically refer to them. Anything you've read as part of your investigation needs to go in the bibliography.

You can make **Citations** in the **Middle** of your **Writing**

1) Citations **refer briefly** to a reference source in the **main body** of your writing.

2) If the citation mentions the **author's name**, you should include the **year** that the work was **published** in brackets.

> This model was found to be suitable at higher levels and was adopted by Alexander (1973).

3) If you do include a citation, you'll need to mention the source **again** at the **end** (in the bibliography, see p. 79), giving the **full details**.

Footnotes allow you to **Add Extra Information**

1) Another way to make references is to use **footnotes**[1], where you place small numbers in the text that lead the reader to the **corresponding number** at the bottom of the page or at the end of the text.

2) Footnote references can refer to **any kind of source** — books, magazines, websites etc. They can also give **extra information** about the point you're trying to make[2].

3) The best thing to do is to keep footnotes **short and sweet**. Long or complicated footnotes take the reader's attention **away** from the main body of your writing and mean they might **lose** the flow of your argument completely.

They were furious that the footnote held no useful information whatsoever.

---

[1] Just like this one. What a fine example.

[2] Keep footnotes in order — the first one on a page is 1, the second is 2, and so on. On the next page you go back to 1.

References and Bibliographies

Bibliographies Reference all your sources In Full

Here's a **sample** of what your bibliography might look like. This example uses the **Harvard Referencing system**. However, there are lots of other systems for referencing, so **check** with your teacher exactly which one you'll be expected to use for your coursework. Whatever style you use, keep all the entries in **alphabetical order**.

Crystal, D. (1995) *The Cambridge Encyclopedia of the English Language*. Cambridge: Cambridge University Press p. 364.

Manches, A. (2008) *Language and Gender — TESOL Talk from Nottingham 07/08*. http://portal.lsri.nottingham.ac.uk/SiteDirectory/TTfN0708/Lists/Posts/Post.aspx?ID=21. Accessed 15/01/2009.

Zimmerman, D. and West, C. (1975) 'Sex roles, interruptions and silences in conversation', in Thorne, B. and Henley, N. [eds] *Language and Sex: Difference and Dominance*. Rowley, Massachusetts: Newbury House pp. 105-29.

Each type of source has to be Referenced in a Certain Way

① Published Books

e.g. Crystal, D. (1995) *The Cambridge Encyclopedia of the English Language*. Cambridge: Cambridge University Press p. 364.

1) All the **published books** that you consulted during the course of your investigation **should be acknowledged**.
2) The correct way of doing this (in the **Harvard** system) is by giving the **name** of the author(s) first — their **surname** followed by the **first letter** of their first name (e.g. Crystal, D. above).
3) Follow the author's name with these details, in this order — **date** of publication, book **title** (in italics), the **city** it was published in and the **publisher**.
4) If you've only used a **section or certain pages** of the book, list these at the **end** of the reference (see above).
5) The bibliography should be arranged in **alphabetical order**, according to the first letter of the author's **surname**.

② Contributions in Other Books / Articles in Magazines or Journals

e.g. Zimmerman, D. and West, C. (1975) 'Sex roles, interruptions and silences in conversation', in Thorne, B. and Henley, N. [eds] *Language and Sex: Difference and Dominance*. Rowley, Massachusetts: Newbury House pp. 105-29.

1) You credit the **author and date** of the article first. Include the **title** of the article in **inverted commas**, and then put the details of the **book**, **magazine** or **journal** in which it appears, in the same way as you would reference any other published book.
2) If you're referencing a magazine or journal, you'll need to include the **volume** and **issue number** (if applicable) **after the title** of the publication itself (e.g. *Journal of Applied Linguistics,* Volume 3, Number 2, pp. 422-436).
3) The general order for referencing **articles** is — **author, date, article title, title of journal** (italics), **volume number, part number, page numbers**. If an article appears in a published book you need to include the **publisher's details**.

③ Websites / Online Resources

e.g. Manches, A. (2008) *Language and Gender — TESOL Talk from Nottingham 07/08*. http://portal.lsri.nottingham.ac.uk/SiteDirectory/TTfN0708/Lists/Posts/Post.aspx?ID=21. Accessed 15/01/2009.

1) If you need to acknowledge a source from **the Internet**, then you have to bear in mind that this material can be **updated** and could have changed **after** you looked at it.
2) You need to give the **URL** (the website's address) so that your source can be **traced**. You can find it in the **address bar** of your web browser. If you're using a lot of websites, make sure you **keep notes** of the addresses.
3) You should reference the **entire address**, starting with *http://*, as above, and put the **date** you looked at the site.
4) On the other hand, if you've consulted a **digital version of a printed publication** (lots of journals etc. are available online), then you should reference these in the **same way** as you would if it was a printed text.

The only source I ever need is ketchup...

Why is it that there's never quite enough in those little pots you get? Why do they do that? If you're not going to provide enough ketchup, then serve fewer chips. Or, shock horror, provide more ketchup, and still serve fewer chips. You'd best learn all this stuff about referencing by the way, before I really go off on one about inverse chip-condiment correlations.

Exam Advice

For your A2 exam, you'll need to understand and apply language frameworks, know how to analyse different types of discourse, organise your answers, write clearly and precisely, and join in on a jolly old language debate along the way. If that's all sounding a bit too much like hard work, then read these exam tips to get you started.

Make sure you know your **Language Frameworks**

Language frameworks can be thought of as **headings** to help you to **structure** your **analysis**. You need to be able to **identify them** in different kinds of texts and explain how the features are used to **create meaning**. So here they are:

> **Language Frameworks**
>
> - **Lexis** (vocabulary)
> - **Semantics** (the meanings that words convey)
> - **Grammar** (word classes, syntax and morphology)
> - **Phonology** (sounds)
> - **Pragmatics** (social conventions surrounding language use)
> - **Graphology** (the visual appearance and arrangement of the text)
> - **Discourse** (how sections of language are developed and structured)

Have a look at section 4 to recap on the language frameworks in more detail, and for specific linguistic terminology.

1) You need to refer to as many of these as possible, as long as they're **appropriate** to the text and the question.

2) Remember to always give examples from the text to support your point, e.g. *Speaker A uses a formal 'title plus surname' address form to address speaker B: 'Mrs Biggs'.*

3) It **doesn't matter** whether you use **single** or **double quotation marks** when you're quoting from the text, as long as you're **consistent**.

4) Don't just be descriptive. You have to relate the frameworks to **purpose** and **meaning**, e.g. *The adjective 'unique' is persuasive, suggesting that the product is special.*

         ↑ **purpose**   ↑ **meaning**

Think about how you're going to **Approach** the **Questions**

All of the exam questions you get will be based around **data**. You might have to write about **written texts**, **spoken material** or **tables** of **data**. When you first open the paper, think about the points on this checklist:

1) Read the **questions** so you know what kind of things to look out for in the texts. Read the texts **quickly** to get a feel for what they're about, then read them again **more carefully** and make brief notes in an essay plan.

2) The best way to prepare is to **underline key features** in the texts you're given.

3) For **written** texts, identify genre, register, likely audience and purpose.

4) For **spoken** texts, identify context, role of participants, register and pragmatics.

5) Find **examples** of the language frameworks — be selective and **link** linguistic features to purpose and meaning.

6) Look for features that **link** the texts (e.g. power, gender, occupation, technology, etc.).

Bear in mind the different **Assessment Objectives**

Assessment objectives are the **criteria** the examiners use to mark your exam answers (and coursework). The number of different AO marks you can get depends on the task.

AO1	You get AO1 marks for using linguistic terminology correctly and writing accurately and effectively.
AO2	You get AO2 marks for showing knowledge of linguistic approaches, and showing that you understand issues related to the construction and analysis of meaning in spoken and written language.
AO3	You get AO3 marks for analysing and evaluating the influence of context on the language used, showing understanding of the key constituents of language.
AO4	You get AO4 marks for using linguistic concepts to show expertise and creativity in your own writing.

Exam Advice

Think about how to **Organise Your Answers**

These are **general guidelines** for how to best cover everything in your answers — if you're asked about something **specific**, you'll have to **tailor** what you say to the particular areas the question asks you to focus on.

Written Discourse	Spoken Discourse
Write a **couple of paragraphs** on: Genre, purpose, register, mode, likely audience.	Write a **couple of paragraphs** on: Context, function, participants.
Write in **more detail** about: **Lexis** (e.g. lexical fields, figurative language) **Grammar** (e.g. word classes — nouns, adverbs etc.) **Discourse structure** (e.g. beginning, development, end) **Phonology** (e.g. alliteration, assonance, repetition) **Graphology** (e.g layout, fonts, images)	Write in **more detail** about: **Non-fluency features** (e.g. pauses, false starts, fillers) **Non-verbal aspects of speech** (e.g. stress) **Pragmatics** (conversational theory) **Phonology** (e.g. pronunciation features) **Lexis**, **grammar** and **discourse structure**.

The A2 exam is **Synoptic**

1) The paper you sit for A2 is **synoptic** — it tests you on the subject as a **whole**.

2) This means that you need to **build on** what you've learnt from **AS**, to show a **broader understanding** of the subject, and recognise when it's **appropriate** to use which bits of information.

3) This is especially the case with your use of **linguistic terminology**. You'll need to be really **familiar** with **specific linguistic terms**, because you're expected to **build** on everything you learnt from AS.

4) All of the questions you'll get will be based on **data**. You need to stay **focused** on this, but use it as a **springboard** for discussing **wider points** about topics you've covered in the rest of the course.

Make sure you know the **Difference** between **Comment** and **Discussion**

1) If you're asked to **comment** on a text, you need to look at the language in **detail**. You'll have to **identify** and **explain** the **key components**.

2) You do this using the **language frameworks** — e.g. you can analyse a text **specifically** in terms of lexis or phonology, or you can do a **broader** analysis where you look at all the relevant frameworks.

3) If you're asked to **discuss** the **issues** in a text, you have to make **judgements** about it. For example, you might comment on the **ideas** that a text raises about a **language debate**, like the superiority of Standard English. You can bring in ideas from **experts** if they help the point you're making.

4) You should analyse specific ideas in the text, using **quotations**. You should then bring in evidence to **support** these ideas, as well as **contrasting points of view**.

"Then Little Red Riding Hood addressed the wolf using the second person pronoun..."

It's **Important** to write **Clearly** and **Precisely**

The points you make need to be as **precise** as possible. There's no need to use **big words** for the sake of it, but it's really important that you use **linguistic terms** appropriately.

1) Spend a few minutes jotting down a **plan** so your answer has some **structure**. Your writing should be **fluent**, so **don't** use **bullet points** in your essay.

2) Write in **paragraphs** and make sure that each paragraph has a clear focus. For example, you might do separate paragraphs on lexis and grammar. **Short sentences** and **paragraphs** are better than long rambling ones.

3) Always use **quotations** and **examples** to **back up** your points. **Short quotations** are better than long ones, and it's good to **weave** them into sentences rather than present them as big separate chunks.

Exam Advice

The A2 exam is **Unit 3, Developing Language**. *(It's possible that the information here could change, so make sure you check the details with your teacher, and read the instructions on the paper carefully on the day.)*

The exam has Two Sections

The exam lasts **two and a half hours** and is split into **two sections**. You need to answer **one** question from **each section**. You should spend **half an hour** reading and preparing the sources, and an **hour** answering **each question**.

Section A — Language Acquisition *[48 marks]*

1) You'll have a choice of **two questions**, each based on a selection of **data**. The data could be things like transcripts of spoken language, or texts written by or for children. It will be based on child language acquisition from **birth** to **eleven years old**.

2) Your answer should **analyse** the children's language development shown in the data. For example, you might analyse the language of two three-year-old children playing.

Section B — Language Change *[48 marks]*

1) For section B you also have a choice of **two questions**, each based on a selection of **data**. The data will be taken from the **Late Modern Period** (from **1700**) to the **present day**.

2) The texts will show evidence of **historical** and **contemporary change** to English, so you need to **analyse** changes in lexis, semantics, grammar, orthography, graphology and discourse structure.

3) You may also have to **discuss** what they show about **issues** like attitudes to language change, the impact of standardisation and how social and political forces can lead to language change.

Here's an **Example Question** and **Answer** to give you some tips:

3   **Text E** is from an article called *Observations in Gardening for January* which appeared in *Gentleman's Magazine* (1731).
   Text F is from a website that gives gardening advice: www.allotment.org (2008).
   • Describe and comment on what these texts show about language change over time.

The texts you'll get in the real exam will be longer than this.

Text E

Lop and top Trees, cut your Coppice and Hedge Rows; in open weather remove and plant Trees and Vines, lay up your Borders, uncover the Roots of Such Trees as require it, putting Soil under them, also prune Vines and Trees, nail and trim wall Fruits, cleanse Trees from Moss and Succors; gather Cions for grafts about the latter end of this month before the Bud sprouts which stick in the ground for some time, because they will take the better for being kept some time from the Tree, graft them the beginning of next month.

Text F

We all know not to plant when it's too wet or too cold, but when we have had a few good days its very difficult to resist popping in a seed or two. How can we be a little more certain whether or not it's ok to start sowing? Well one sure test is the "**baby water test**". Yes, place your elbow in the soil and if it's too cold you will soon know it. Just like baby's bath water your elbow makes a great tester to check if the soil is suitable or not. Your fingers and hands are just not suitable for either task.

Text E has some eighteenth century orthographical features, for example the capitalisation of proper nouns: 'Vines and Trees'. The syntax is complex and contains lots of subordinate clauses. Lexical change can be seen in the division of the now compound noun 'hedgerows' into two separate words: 'Hedge Rows'.

Good use of language frameworks

Identifies similarities in the texts

Both texts address the reader directly with the second person pronoun 'you'. This draws readers in and makes them more likely to take the advice. Text F also uses the plural pronoun 'we', to make readers feel included, and uses interrogatives: 'How can we be a little more certain whether or not it's ok to start sowing?'.

Makes direct contrasts between the two texts

Discusses the effect of certain language features

Text F has a less formal tone than Text E. It uses features of spoken language, for example the informal present participle 'popping'. The syntax is less complex — there are fewer subordinate clauses and sentences are shorter. It's also less authoritative than Text E — there is only one imperative ('place your elbow...') compared to numerous ones in Text E (e.g. 'nail and trim'). It's typical of the period Text E was written in that it sounds more authoritative than friendly....

This answer covers **lexis** and **grammar** well. There is effective use of **linguistic terminology**, particularly when discussing **grammar**. There's **good comparison** between the two texts. **Quotations** are used to support most points, and the examples are **well-integrated** into the main body of the answer. Some parts of the answer, e.g. the point about complex syntax, need to be **supported** by **quotations** from the text. The essay should go on to discuss other language frameworks, such as semantics and discourse structure. This is only a partial answer, but the essay would get about **39 marks** out of **48** if it kept up this standard all the way through.

Answers to Exam Questions

This answer section gives you some tips about what to include when you have a go at the sample exam questions at the end of sections 1 to 3. We haven't written complete essays (everyone writes essays differently), but these points are suggestions for the things you should include in your answers.

Section 1 — Language Acquisition

Pages 18-19

1   The question asks you to comment on the texts in terms of language acquisition and discuss how the child is being helped to understand what happens in the story. Here are some points you could include in your answer:

Text A — conversation between Ellie and her mother

- In text A, Ellie's mother is making sure that Ellie understands the story. Ellie's mother is the main contributor, which is to be expected, as early conversations are usually initiated and maintained by adults. Ellie's contributions to the conversation are mainly short statements that her mother responds to.

- The mother uses direct questions (e.g. *what's that in her hand*) and imperatives (e.g. *look*). She also uses tag questions: *you brush your teeth don't you*, and addresses Ellie directly. These devices are used to encourage Ellie to respond. She gives positive feedback to encourage pragmatic development and make sure that Ellie keeps giving answers, e.g. *very good*. The mother also maintains the conversation by repeating what Ellie says, e.g. *ooh yes look at all the bubbles*. These are all features of child-directed speech. Ellie's comments are expanded by her mother to further encourage her development: the utterance *and she's got water* is expanded to *yes you're right she's all wet isn't she (.) she's gone to wash her face*.

- The mother uses the story as something to base a dialogue on — she uses it to prompt discussion, rather than just reading it out in full. This is probably partly because Ellie is too young to be able to follow the words properly.

- Ellie doesn't always respond to what her mother says. She points out things that she finds interesting, and her mother follows her lead and then brings the conversation back to the topic. This shows that Ellie is still learning how to take part in a dialogue, which is typical for a 3-year-old. She is able to take turns most of the time though, and seems to understand adjacency pairs. For example, when her mother asks the question: *what's that in her hand*, Ellie replies: *she's got her (.) toothbrush*.

- Ellie's speech is typical of a 3-year-old's. She's able to use some full sentences, e.g. *I can't see her teeth*. She can also ask questions using *wh-* words and auxiliary verbs: *what is it on the next one*. She shows some inconsistent usage of inflections, e.g. using *got* and *gotted*. She also has difficulty pronouncing consonant clusters. This is cluster reduction, e.g. she says *plish* instead of *splish* because it's easier.

Text B — extract from an illustrated children's story

- The story is child-focused — it's based on a topic that a young child could recognise and relate to. It's also about simple actions and concrete things that the child could see and touch, e.g. a toothbrush.

- The sentences in the extract are simple — they're mostly short, single clauses, e.g. *She liked to have a big stretch every morning*. The coordinating conjunction *and* is used, which children usually become familiar with quite quickly and tend to find easy to use.

- Most of the words are monosyllabic, e.g. *jumped out of bed*. This makes them easier for a child to understand and pronounce. There's a lot of repetition, e.g. the verb *to wash* is used three times. This gives children a chance to become familiar with a word, rather than being confused by lots of synonyms.

- The story also contains some phonological devices, which make the language more interesting. For example, onomatopoeia is used to describe Rosie washing her face: *Splish, splash, splosh!* This mimics the kind of child-directed speech that Ellie's mother uses. It lends itself to the exaggerated intonation that lots of adults use when they talk to children — Ellie's mother emphasises these words, as well as the words *big dollop*. Phonological features also encourage interaction, as the child can join in and enjoy making unusual sounds.

Section 2 — Language Change

Pages 36-37

1   The question asks you to analyse both texts in terms of what they show about the changes in written language over time. Here are some points you could make in your answer:

Text A — from *The First Book of Manners*

- The syntax in this text is quite complex, which is typical of English from the Victorian period. It contains a lot of subordinate clauses: *should it be your duty, perform it reverently, with a due feeling of devotion*. The opening sentence appears archaic to a modern reader because it begins with a subordinate clause and is in the passive: *When the hour for meals draws nigh*. However, because this was written for children, the language isn't as complex as a text written for adults from the same period. Most of the clauses are quite straightforward, even though the sentences are long: *You will find the knife and spoon at your right hand...*

- The lexis is also formal compared with Present Day English. It contains more Latinate words than text B, e.g. *ascribed, unmannerly*. There is also nineteenth century spelling, e.g. *Shew* (in modern texts it would be *show*) and *unfrequently* (instead of *infrequently*).

- The text is quite heavily punctuated and semi-colons are frequently used, whereas in more modern texts they are quite unusual, e.g. the writer uses one in *shew no*

Answers to Exam Questions

unbecoming haste to sit down; but take your place...
Placing a semi-colon before a coordinating conjunction is rare in modern texts.

- By addressing the reader directly using the second person pronoun *you* and possessive pronoun *your*, the writer creates a sense of a formal lecture. It's as if the reader is being directly spoken to by the writer. If it had been in the third person then the writer would seem more detached.

- The writer assumes the role of an expert, using imperatives like *Sit upright* to instruct the reader. He is very prescriptive about the way the reader should act, for example, the use of the modal verb *will* in *You will find the knife and spoon* creates an authoritative and definite tone.

- The text aims to educate the reader about a strict hierarchy — there is a *head of the family* or *clergyman* in charge, and the *youngest present* is expected to perform their duties *reverently*.

Text B — from a website for parents

- This text is an extract from a twentieth century website giving advice to parents about how to get their children to conduct themselves at mealtimes.

- As in text A the writer addresses the reader directly using *you* and *your*: *Find out which rules work for you.* They also use imperatives like *serve, give,* and *assure* to come across as knowledgeable and authoritative.

- The writer uses direct statements to persuade the reader into accepting a shared understanding of proper behaviour (*No one wants to see what's in their mouths*).

- The lexis in text B is not as formal as it is in the nineteenth century text (it includes informal terms like *kids* and adjectives like *crazy*) and includes exclamatory sentences: *piling a plate with a mountain of food is a recipe for frustrations!*). This is intended to show the process as having an element of entertainment and fun about it, as well as making it seem like the writer is using the voice of experience. The text contains metaphor (*ravenous monsters*), which makes it more entertaining and informal. This effect is emphasised by the use of phonological features, e.g. assonance in *Chow Down* and alliteration in *Chew and Chat*.

- The sentences in the text are of varying complexity. The writer uses conditional clauses to pre-empt how the children in question might behave, e.g. *If they need to remove something from their mouth*, which also suggests they've experienced the same thing. It puts them at the same level as the reader, rather than dictating strict rules like the author of text A.

- The punctuation of the text reflects the relative unpopularity of semi-colons in modern written English compared to the Victorian English in text A. The writer in text B uses commas, full stops and colons.

- Rather than being in linked paragraphs like text A, this text is broken down into sections with individual headings, and uses bullet points to make lists. This is intended to make it easier for the reader to digest the information as it's in smaller, manageable blocks. This is typical of the layout of web-based texts, and shows a more modern, informal style than text A.

2   This question also asks you to comment on how the language in each of the texts reflects the development of language over time. Here are a few things you could discuss in your answer:

Text C — a letter by Byron (1819)

- Text C has a very personal, intimate tone, and includes terms of endearment like *my love*, and *dearest Teresa*, suggesting that the purpose of the letter is to convey Byron's affection. The personal nature of the text is intensified by the frequent use of the personal pronouns *I, me* and *you*.

- The letter mainly uses the simple present tense, which also intensifies the sentiments contained in it. There is a sense of immediacy to Byron's writing, e.g. *I feel, I love, I wish that*. This makes the reader feel as if they're being spoken to directly.

- There isn't much archaic lexis in the letter, other than the use of *hereafter*, which is a compound that isn't often used in English any more. The lexis is occasionally complex, e.g. *comprised, cease*, but is generally the same as you would expect from any personal letter written in Standard English for a known audience.

- However one common feature of older texts is that they have quite complicated syntax, making them seem much more formal than modern texts. For example, this letter contains several coordinate or subordinate clauses in one sentence, e.g. the sentence that begins *But you will recognize....*

- Byron also uses a shorter sentence to conclude the letter and some shorter clauses towards the end of it. The final sentence, which begins with an imperative: *Think of me*, has a very direct impact and ensures the letter stays in the reader's mind.

Text D — a letter from 1972

- This text seems less emotive than text C, despite also having a very personal tone. It's similar to text C in that it also uses the second person pronoun *you* to directly address the reader.

- The letter is in a different style from text C. It engages with the reader in a familiar, conversational manner without any of the wild or intense declarations of love or feelings that mark Byron's letter.

- The lexis is not quite as formal as Byron's, and has some quite informal turns of phrase like the noun phrase *terrible wimp* and the colloquial verb phrase *stuck in to*. A lot of the lexis is in the lexical field of travel, e.g. adjectives like *jetlagged*. This shows the impact of technology on Present Day English, as this word wouldn't have been available to Byron in the early nineteenth century.

Answers to Exam Questions

- The writing is conversational and regularly self-referential (e.g. *yes, that's me talking*). It maintains its informal style with contractions like *I've, I'm, can't* and *till*. This marks it out as a Present Day English text, as contractions were used much less in the nineteenth century. It also contains ellipsis: *will write again soon*.

- Text D is similar to text C in its ending — the writer also uses imperatives to make the sentiments more direct (*Give my love, tell them I'm fine*).

Section 3 — Attitudes towards Language

Pages 44-45

3   This question asks you to discuss the ideas contained in the two texts using your knowledge of language change, and to comment on the type of language used. Here are some points you could pick out to talk about in your answer:

Text A — from the Preface to Johnson's Dictionary

- Johnson's ideas about language change were based upon the fact that he thought English needed to be recorded, regulated and controlled. He recognises how important the role of language was in the *cultivation* of literature, but then says that as the language grew it became *neglected* and corrupted by people not using it properly (*ignorance*), and the unpredictable ways that people created new phrases (*caprices of innovation*).

- This shows that Johnson was a prescriptivist — his aim was to create an *established principle* by which words or phrases used in English could be *rejected or received*.

- Johnson recognises that there's a difference between distinguishing the *irregularities that are inherent* in English from the features that have come about through *ignorance or negligence*. This shows some agreement with text B, as there's an acceptance that languages always change and will never be completely consistent.

- However, text A differs from text B because Johnson makes value judgements about which features are *improprieties* and *absurdities* that he feels it is his *duty... to correct or proscribe*.

- The language of this text is typical of eighteenth century English. The sentences are long and the syntax is complex — there are lots of subordinate clauses separated by commas and semi-colons. The lexis is formal and there are a lot of Latinate words, e.g. *perplexity, tyranny*. There is also some archaic spelling, e.g. *energetick*.

Text B — from *The language web*, by Jean Aitchison

- In contrast to Johnson, Aitchison is in favour of describing linguistic change, rather than trying to regulate it. She states that *Naturally, language changes all the time*, and contrasts this descriptive approach with the more extreme attitude that change represents *decay*.

- Aitchison makes her feelings about the linguists who identify aspects of language as *deformed or bad* pretty clear, comparing them with out of touch *cranks who argue that the world is flat*. This suggests that she thinks prescriptivism is archaic compared to the descriptive approach of the majority of modern linguists.

- She attributes the concerns other people have about language change being a bad thing to *traditional* feelings. She argues that it's a stage that each generation seems to pass through as they become worried about protecting the conventions of language that they learned as they grew up.

- Aitchison also highlights how the notion of *correct* English was often related to how the members of the *upper- and middle-class* would speak, as well as the influence of Latin. She mentions how Latin was prestigious at the time of the first prescriptivists, due to its fixed grammar. There is evidence for this view in text A — Johnson talks about *writers of classical reputation or acknowledged authority*, showing how the idea behind prescriptive attitudes was to copy what was seen as a rigid model of language that guaranteed prestige.

- Aitchison's language is generally quite informal, and she tries to balance both sides of the argument by giving the history and motivations behind prescriptive views. However she disagrees with them through direct statements like *'correct English' was as hard to define then as it is now*, and by asking rhetorical questions, e.g. *Is our language really changing for the worse, as some people argue?*

Glossary

abstract noun A **noun** that refers to a concept, state, quality or emotion.

accent The distinctive way a speaker from a particular region pronounces words.

acronym A new word made from the initial letters of all the words in a name or **phrase**, e.g NASA.

active voice When the **subject** of the sentence is directly performing the **verb** e.g. *Steve burst the bubble.*

adjacency pair Dialogue that follows a set pattern, e.g. when speakers greet each other.

adjective A class of words that can appear before (attributive) or after (predicative) a **noun** to describe it, e.g. *pretty.*

adverb A class of words that modify **verbs** according to time, place, manner, frequency, duration or degree. They can also sometimes modify nouns and adjectives too.

affixation The process of adding an affix before (**prefix**) or after (**suffix**) an existing word to change either its meaning or grammatical function.

alliteration When two or more words close to each other in a **phrase** begin with the same sound, e.g. *down in the dumps.*

allusion When a text or speaker refers to a saying, idea, etc. outside the text or conversation.

amelioration When a word develops a more positive meaning over time.

antonyms Words with opposite meanings.

archaism An old-fashioned word or phrase that isn't used in Present Day English, e.g. *forsooth.*

article A kind of **determiner** that shows if the reference to a **noun** is general (*a / an*) or specific (*the*).

aspect A **verb's** aspect shows whether the action it refers to is already completed, or if it is still taking place.

assimilation When sounds next to each other in a spoken word or **sentence** are pronounced in a different way from normal to make them easier to say.

assonance When the main vowel sounds of two or more words that are close together in a text are similar or the same, e.g. *low smoky holes.*

audience A person or group of people that read, view or listen to a text or performance. A writer or speaker can aim to appeal to a certain type of audience by using specific literary techniques and language choices.

auxiliary verbs Verbs used before the **main verb** in a sentence to give extra information about it, e.g. *I have seen him.*

babbling The production of short vowel / consonant combinations by a baby acquiring language.

back-formation In word formation, back-formation occurs when it looks like a **suffix** has been added to an existing base form to create a new word, but in fact the suffix has been removed to create a new term e.g. the **verb** *enthuse* was formed from the **noun** *enthusiast.*

behaviourism A theory of language acquisition that suggests children learn language through a process of imitation and reinforcement.

bidialectism The ability of speakers to switch between two **dialect** forms, the most common being between **Standard English** and a speaker's regional variety.

blending When parts of two words are combined to make a new one, e.g. *netizen.*

borrowing When words from one language fall into common usage in another as a result of contact.

broadening When a word that has quite a specific meaning becomes more general over time (also called generalisation, expansion or extension).

child-directed speech (CDS) The way that caregivers talk to children — usually in simplified and / or exaggerated language.

clause The simplest meaningful unit of a **sentence**.

cliché A expression that has lost its novelty value due to being overused.

clipping When a shortened version of a word becomes a word in its own right, e.g. *demo, phone.*

Glossary

cluster reduction When a child only pronounces one consonant from a consonant cluster, e.g. saying *pay* instead of *play*.

cognitive theory A theory of language acquisition that suggests children need to have developed certain mental abilities before they can acquire language.

coining The general term for creating new words.

collective noun A **noun** that refers to a group of people, animals or things, e.g. *team*.

colloquialism An informal word or phrase that wouldn't normally be used in formal written English, e.g. *How's it going, mate?*

common noun A **noun** that refers to a class of things or a concept. Every noun is a common noun except those that refer to unique things, e.g. the names of particular people or places.

comparative An **adjective** that makes a degree of comparison, normally by adding an -*er* **suffix**, e.g. *faster*.

complement A word or **phrase** that gives more information about the **subject** or **object** in a sentence, e.g. *the boy is actually a cow*.

compound A new word created by combining two or more existing words, e.g. *skyscraper*.

concrete noun A **noun** that refers to things you can physically touch or see, e.g. *chair*.

conjunction A linking word that connects **phrases** and **clauses** to each other to form **sentences**, e.g. *but*.

connotation The associations that are made with a particular word.

context The circumstances that surround a word, **phrase** or text, e.g. time and place produced, intended audience.

contraction A word that's formed by shortening and combining two or more words, e.g. *can't, might've*.

conversion When a word becomes part of a different **word class** in addition to its original sense (e.g. *text* is now both a **noun** and a **verb**).

cooing The earliest sounds children are able to make as they experiment with moving their lips and tongue.

coordinate clause An independent **clause** that's linked to another independent **clause** in the same **sentence**.

coordinating conjunction A linking word like *and*, *but* and *or* that connects independent phrases and **clauses** to each other, e.g. *He was handsome and she was jolly.*

count noun A **noun** that can be preceded by a number and counted, e.g. *one book, two books* etc.

Critical Period Hypothesis A theory popularised by Lenneberg (1967), which states that if a child does not have any linguistic interaction before the ages of 5-6, their language development will be severely limited.

declarative sentence A **sentence** that makes a statement to give information, e.g. *she enjoyed her scampi.*

deixis A reference to something outside of the text or conversation (e.g. location, time) that can't be understood unless you know the **context**.

deletion When a child misses out consonants in words, e.g. saying *sto* instead of *stop*.

demonstrative Words that refer to specific objects that only those involved in the discourse can see. They can be **pronouns**, e.g. *I like this*, or **adjectives**, e.g. *I like this bike.*

denotation The literal meaning of a word.

descriptivism The attitude that no use of language is incorrect and that variation should be acknowledged and recorded rather than corrected.

determiner A word that goes before a **noun** to show possession or number (e.g. *his, two*).

dialect The distinctive **lexis**, **grammar** and pronunciation of a person's spoken English, usually affected by the region they're from and their social background.

dialect levelling A process of **language contact** where differences between **dialects** in proximity to each other are gradually lost.

Glossary

diphthong Two vowel sounds that are joined together to form one sound, e.g. the *a* in *late* is a diphthong as it starts with an /e/ phoneme and finishes on an /ɪ/.

discourse An extended piece of written or spoken language.

double comparative Using an **adjective** that makes a degree of comparison, normally by adding an -*er* **suffix**, with the word *more*, e.g. *more faster*.

double negative When negatives are used twice in a phrase, e.g. *I didn't do nothing*.

egocentric The early mental state of a child in which they can only understand things existing in relation to themselves, i.e. things they can see or touch, etc.

elision When sounds or **syllables** are left out in speech to make pronunciation easier and quicker. They end up sounding like they're slurred together, e.g. *d'ya* instead of *do you*.

ellipsis When part of a grammatical structure is left out of the **sentence** without affecting the meaning.

Estuary English An **accent** that was originally from the Thames Estuary area in London but is now heard outside the area and may be replacing **RP** as the country's most widespread form.

euphemism A word or phrase that is used as a substitute for harsher or more unpleasant sounding words or concepts.

exclamative A **sentence** that has an expressive function and ends with an exclamation mark.

figurative language Language that is used in a non-literal way to create images and form comparisons, e.g. metaphor and simile.

filler A sound produced by speakers to keep a conversation going and avoid silence, e.g. *mm*.

fricative A group of consonant sounds in English produced by forcing air through a restricted passage (e.g. between the lips or teeth). Some of the English fricatives are *th* sounds, *f*, *v*, *s*, *z*, *j* sounds, and *sh* sounds.

genre A group of texts with a particular form or purpose, e.g. letters, poems, adverts.

glottal stop A sound produced when the vocal cords interrupt the flow of air, often to replace a /t/ sound (e.g. *water* becomes *wa-uh*).

grammar The system of rules that governs how **words**, **clauses** and **sentences** are put together.

graphology The study of the appearance of a text, how it looks on the page and how the layout helps to get the meaning across.

head word A word that has the same grammatical function as the **phrase** that has been built around it, e.g. in a noun phrase, the head word is a **noun**.

holophrase In language acquisition, a single word that expresses a complete idea, e.g. *ball*, which could mean the child wants it, or has found it, etc. Caregivers need contextual clues to interpret holophrases.

hyperbole When exaggeration is used for effect.

idiom A saying that doesn't make sense if interpreted literally but is understood because it's commonly used e.g. *I could eat a horse*.

imagery Describing something in a way that creates a picture of it in the mind of an audience.

imperative A **sentence** that gives orders, advice or directions. It starts with a **main verb** and doesn't have a **subject**.

implication When a meaning is suggested, rather than explicitly described.

infinitive The base form of a **verb**, preceded by *to*, e.g. *to sing*.

inflection An **affix** that is attached to a base word and gives extra information about it, e.g. its tense or person.

initialism Where the first letter of a word stands for the word itself as part of an abbreviation e.g. *FBI* (for Federal Bureau of Investigation). Initialisms are always pronounced letter by letter.

Glossary

internalisation When a child learning language starts to apply one of the language's rules consistently, even to words they've never seen before.

interrogative A sentence or utterance that asks a question.

intertextuality When a text makes reference to another existing text for effect.

intonation The pitch of a speaker's voice, e.g. rising intonation shows it's a question.

jargon 1. The chattering sounds that babies make before they start using proper words. It sounds like a made-up language.
2. Specialist words that are used by a particular social or occupational group that may not be understood by a non-member.

language acquisition device (LAD) The innate ability of children acquiring language to take in and use the grammatical rules of the language they hear, according to Chomsky (1965).

language acquisition support system (LASS) The system of support from caregivers to children that helps them to acquire language and become sociable, according to Bruner (1983).

language contact Occurs when speakers of different languages or varieties of the same language interact for prolonged periods.

Late Modern English The more **standardised** form of the English language, used from around 1700.

lexical field A group of words that relate to the same topic, e.g. *hotel* and *destination* are in the lexical field of travel.

lexis A general term for the words of a language.

liaison When a consonant is pronounced between words or **syllables** to make them run together.

lingua franca A language used for communication between speakers who don't have the same native language.

loan words Words that are taken from other languages.

main verb A word that identifies the action of a **sentence**.

mass noun A **noun** that can't be counted and doesn't have a plural, e.g. *information*.

metaphor Words or phrases that describe something as if it was actually something else, e.g. *the heart of the matter*.

metonymy Using a part of something, or one of its attributes, to describe the whole thing, e.g. *the press* to refer to journalists and the news industry.

modal auxiliary verbs Verbs that give more information about the **main verb**, but can't occur as main verbs themselves, e.g. *can*, *will*.

mode A way of classifying texts, e.g. written or spoken or a combination of the two.

modifier A word, usually an **adjective** or **adverb**, that changes (modifies) the meaning of a **head word**.

monosyllabic Words with only one **syllable**.

morpheme The individual meaningful units that make up words (although they can't always stand alone).

morphology The study of the internal structure of words.

multimodal text A text that involves elements of different **modes**, e.g. text messages are a mixture of written and spoken language.

narrative voice The point of view a text is written from, e.g. a first person narrator tells the story from their personal point of view.

narrowing When a word that has a general meaning becomes more specific over time (also called specialisation or restriction).

negatives Words like *not* and *no*, that turn positive statements into negative ones, e.g. *I'm not here tomorrow*.

neologisms New words that enter a language.

non-fluency features Features that interrupt the flow of talk, e.g. hesitation, repetition, **fillers**, interruption and overlap.

Glossary

non-verbal communication Any method of communication that isn't words, e.g. gestures, facial expressions, body language and tone of voice.

noun A word used as the name of a person, place, thing or concept.

object The part of the **sentence** that the **verb** acts upon, e.g. in *I broke a plate*, the plate is the object and ends up *broken*.

omission When sounds are left out from words. If a lot of speakers do this over a prolonged period of time, the sound can end up being lost altogether.

onomatopoeia A word that sounds like the noise it's describing, e.g. *buzz*.

orthography The writing system of a language — how the language is represented through symbols (letters) and spelling.

overextension When a child acquiring language uses a word too generally to refer to different but related things, e.g. calling everything with four legs a *dog*.

oxymoron A phrase that brings two conflicting ideas together, e.g. *bittersweet*.

parentheses Another word for brackets.

parody Subverting traditional expectations of a text's features to produce humour or satire.

passive voice When the **object** of the verb is described first, rather than the **subject** (e.g. *the bubble* was burst by Steve).

pejoration When a word develops a more negative meaning over time.

personification When an object, concept or situation is given human qualities.

phatic language Expressions that have a social function rather than expressing serious meaning, e.g *hello*.

phoneme The smallest unit of sound.

phonemic contraction When a baby stops making certain sounds, and just makes the sounds it hears from the language its caregivers use. This happens at about 10 months.

phonemic expansion When a baby starts to make lots of different sounds in the babbling stage. This occurs before **phonemic contraction**.

phonetics The study of how speech sounds are made and received.

phonology The study of the sound systems of languages, in particular the patterns of sounds.

phrase A meaningful unit of language built around a **head word**.

plosive A consonant sound in English produced by completely stopping the flow of air from the lungs and then releasing it. English plosives include *p*, *b*, *t*, *d*, *k*, and *g*.

political correctness Avoiding using language or ideas that might be offensive about members of a particular group (e.g. ethnic, gender, or age groups).

polysyllabic Words with more than one **syllable**.

post-modifiers Words that come after the **head word** in a **phrase** and tell you something about it.

pragmatics The study of how language functions in social situations.

pre-modifiers Words used before the head word of a **phrase** (often **determiner** + **adjective**) that tell you something about it.

prefix An **affix** that comes before the base form, e.g. *unfortunate*.

preposition A word that defines the relationship between things in terms of time, space or direction, e.g. *the toy was in the box*, *he's behind you*.

prescriptivism The attitude that language should have a strict set of rules that must be obeyed in speech and writing.

primary auxiliary verbs **Auxiliary verbs** that can also occur as **main verbs** (*do*, *be* and *have*).

pronoun A word that can take the place of a **noun**, e.g. *he*, *she*, *it*.

Glossary

proper noun A **noun** that is the name of a specific person, place or brand.

prosody **Non-verbal** aspects of speech like pace, stress, pitch, intonation, volume and pauses.

proto-word A combination of sounds that a child uses that actually contains meaning, rather than just being a random utterance like **cooing** or **babbling**.

pun Replacing a word or phrase with one that sounds the same or similar for creative or humorous effect.

quantifier A word that gives information about the quantity of a **noun**, e.g. *there are a few cardigans*.

Received Pronunciation (RP) An **accent** traditionally associated with educated people and the upper class. It's characterised by lots of long vowels and the pronunciation of /h/ and /t/ in words where people with regional accents might leave them out.

register A type of language that's appropriate for a particular audience or situation, e.g. formal language is appropriate for a political speech.

sans-serif typeface A typeface where there aren't any fine 'strokes' attached to the tops and bottoms of letters.

schwa A generic vowel sound ([ə]) that is usually pronounced in unstressed syllables e.g. the e in *system* or the *a* in *alone*.

semantics The study of how the meanings of words are created and interpreted.

sentence An independent grammatical unit made up of one or more **clauses**.

serif typeface A typeface where fine 'strokes' are attached to the tops and bottoms of letters.

similes Comparisons that use the words *like* or *as*.

simplification When a child learning to speak drops consonants or consonant clusters to make words easier to pronounce, or swaps the consonants for others that are easier to pronounce.

slang Informal, non-standard vocabulary used in casual speech.

split infinitive When the base form of a verb is separated from the word *to* by another word — usually an adverb, e.g. *to quickly run*.

Standard English A **dialect** of English considered 'correct' and 'normal', because it has distinctive and standardised features of spelling, vocabulary and **syntax**. It's the form of English usually used in formal writing.

standardisation The process by which grammarians and prescriptivists attempted to structure and influence English usage according to what they believed constituted 'correct' or 'incorrect' usage of the language.

subject The focus of a **sentence** — the person or thing that performs the action described by the **verb**, e.g. *Billy ate a sandwich*.

subordinate clause A **clause** that gives extra information about the main clause, but can't stand alone and still make sense.

subordinating conjunction A linking word like *although* or *because* that connects a subordinate clause to the main clause, e.g. *I'm off work because I feel sick*.

substitution When a child replaces a consonant in a word with one that's easier to say, e.g. saying *dot* instead of *got*.

subtext The implied meaning behind what's actually being said or described.

suffix An **affix** that comes after the base form, e.g. *sadness*.

superlative An **adjective** that states the **noun** it's describing is beyond comparison. It's formed by adding -est, e.g. *fastest*, or using the word *most*, e.g. *most beautiful*.

syllables The individual units of pronunciation that make up a word.

symbolism When a word or phrase represents something other than its literal meaning.

Glossary

synonyms Words that have the same or very similar meanings.

syntax The order and structure of sentences.

tag question A question added to the end of a statement to encourage a response, e.g. *don't you think so?*

telegraphic stage The stage of language acquisition at which children begin to create three- or four-word utterances containing mainly **subjects**, **verbs**, **objects** and **complements**.

tense Grammatical **inflections** on verbs that show the time an action took place, e.g. in the past or present.

th-fronting When a speaker replaces *th*-sounds with *f* or *v*, e.g. *think* as *fink* and *them* as *vem*.

underextension When a child uses words in a very restricted way, e.g. using a word like *hat* to refer only to the one the child is wearing, not to other hats too.

uptalk / upspeak When the intonation rises at the end of statements rather than just questions.

verb A word that describes the action or state that a **sentence** refers to.

vernacular The commonly-spoken language of a country or region.

word classes How words are categorised according to the function they can perform in a **sentence**.

Zone of Proximal Development Vygotsky's (1978) theory that when caregivers help children with verbal responses, they provide a model that the child can copy and apply when they're in other situations.

Index